The

EVERYTHING® Paying for College Book

Dear Reader:

You may be dreaming of a college education. But if your situation is anything like ours was, the high cost is making you wonder if you can possibly afford it. Through our experience and careers in higher education, we have learned that students can pay for college in many ways. All students' abilities and situations are different; however, there is a way for every student to find the money to pay for college.

Besides students, parents will also find plenty of useful information in this book. Whether you are the parent of a very young child or you already have a child in college, you can take steps now to help pay for your student's college education. Investigating the myriad financial aid options in this book is a great start.

We hope you discover the particular combination of resources to make your dream of a college education a reality. Remember that there is always a path leading in the direction you want to travel. The only thing that matters is that you keep searching. It may require time and hard work on your part, but the doors of opportunity a college degree opens will make the work worthwhile!

Sheryle A. Proper

An Everything® Series Book.
Everything® and everything.com® are registered trademarks of F+W Publications, Inc.

Published by Adams Media, an F+W Publications Company
57 Littlefield Street, Avon, MA 02322 U.S.A.
www.adamsmedia.com

ISBN: 1-59337-300-7
Printed in the United States of America.

J I H G F E D C B A

Library of Congress Cataloging-in-Publication Data
Brown, Nathan.
The everything paying for college book / by Nathan Brown and Sheryle A. Proper.
p. cm.
(An everything series book)
ISBN 1-59337-300-7
1. College costs--United States. 2. Student aid--United States. 3. Education, Higher--United States--Finance. I. Proper, Sheryle A. II. Title. III. Series: Everything series.

LB2342.B75 2005
378.3'8--dc22
2004025951

This publication is designed to provide accurate and authoritative information with regard to the subject matter covered. It is sold with the understanding that the publisher is not engaged in rendering legal, accounting, or other professional advice. If legal advice or other expert assistance is required, the services of a competent professional person should be sought.

—From a *Declaration of Principles* jointly adopted by a Committee of the American Bar Association and a Committee of Publishers and Associations

Many of the designations used by manufacturers and sellers to distinguish their products are claimed as trademarks. Where those designations appear in this book and Adams Media was aware of a trademark claim, the designations have been printed with initial capital letters.

This book is available at quantity discounts for bulk purchases.
For information, call 1-800-872-5627.

Contents

Dedications and Acknowledgments

To my husband, Wendell, who took on more than his share of responsibility around the house so I could pursue my bachelor's and master's degrees, and to the college students I am most proud of, our sons: Andy, a graduate of Messiah College, and Matt, a student at Pennsylvania State University.

Special thanks to my professors and coworkers at Allegheny College, who share my love of learning, and to my colleagues at PASFAA, who have taught me much about the field of student financial aid.

~Sheryle Proper

To my daughter, Faith Brown, who was unborn as I wrote this but will be born before it sees print—Faith, I haven't even had a chance to teach you anything yet, but you've already taught me so much. I hope can be as good a father as you deserve. This is also dedicated to the beautiful mother of my child, Amanda Harper, who is likely chasing me and Faith down at this very moment. Now she has two children to keep track of.

Thanks to everyone at Adams Media, especially editors Kate Burgo and Christina MacDonald, for all the patience, cooperation, and all the hard work they put into this book. This was no easy task for anyone, and I could not have gotten through it without you.

~Nathan Brown

Top Ten Things You Should Know

About Paying for College

1. If you know where to look and how to apply, you are likely to find money that you won't have to repay!
2. It's best to think of paying for college as a team endeavor, with students, parents, and financial aid administrators working together to find the most effective combination of resources.
3. Working doesn't necessarily detract from a student's education. Many employment opportunities accommodate academic obligations—and may even enhance the student's academic interests.
4. Start a microinvesting program when your child is young to accumulate substantial resources to put toward college.
5. Don't rule out any college or university because of cost. What really matters is the net cost you will have to pay, not the "sticker price" of the institution.
6. Students should take part in activities that are important to them, not that they think will be important to administrators.
7. Some students have to include loans when they pay for college costs. The future opportunities created by the education will pay for the loan many times over.
8. Financial aid opportunities continue to become available throughout the time students are in college. Don't stop looking for them.
9. To maximize your potential for admission and financial aid, there are things you should (and shouldn't) say when completing applications.
10. Anyone who wants a college education can afford one.

Introduction

▶ There are dozens of reasons for choosing to pursue a college education. Parents also have a number of reasons to want their children to earn a degree. As a prospective student, your reasons may be as personal as broadening your horizons or as sensible as acquiring the vocational skills needed in order to enter (or return to) the workforce after receiving your degree. Regardless of your reasons for going to college, whether you plan to seek admission to an Ivy League school, a state university, or the local community college, you will have no choice but to face up to one cold, hard fact. Someone, somehow, will have to pay for your higher education! Unless you are fortunate enough to already have a trust fund, a college fund, or a parent (or other rich relative) who is willing and able to pay your way, that "someone" is probably going to be you. (Parents, if you're trying to plan ahead so you *can* be the willing-and-able one, don't worry—this book has plenty of advice for you, too!)

Though it is a somewhat safer environment than the "real world," college should be seen as a four-year crash-course introduction to understanding how the world operates. A higher education will provide you with much more than just a piece of paper proving you earned a degree. If you are entering college straight out of high school, it will give you your first experiences of how life will work without mom and dad. No one will be able to write you a note if you forget (or just fail) to do an assignment or meet a responsibility. The ball will be in your hands, more so than it has ever been before. With the stress of classes, reading assignments, midterms, final exams, and term papers on your mind, the last thing you (or any college student, for that matter) need are financial worries stacked on top of the academic ones.

To be accepted to the schools of their choice, it is important for today's prospective college students to earn more than the minimum required GPA. Similarly, if they plan to meet the financial obligations of rising tuition and inflated living expenses, along with high-priced course textbooks and required supplies, college students must also be equipped with a working understanding of how money comes and goes out in the big, bad world.

Financially speaking, we live in a very difficult time for college students. As government funding is increasingly cut from colleges and universities, more and more academic institutions are finding themselves with no alternative but to hike the cost of tuition. Unfortunately, this translates into a heavier monetary burden for both current and prospective college students.

But please don't let that discourage you. No matter how grim you may think your chances are for paying for college, things are not as bad as they seem. There is still hope, and it starts right here between the covers of this book! With *The Everything® Paying for College Book*, you will take a guided tour through a vast arsenal of possible weapons to help you (and/or your parents) battle your way toward paying for college, from methods as solid as finding ways to capitalize on your academic and other merit-based strengths, to tactics as creative as microinvesting or even starting your own business. As we cover these potential strategies, we also provide you with the know-how that will empower you to make your own decision on the avenue of attack most appropriate for your own unique situation.

Whether you are a returning, nontraditional prospective student without a dime to spare to pay for grad school, a recent or soon-to-be high school graduate without enough money to go to the college of your dreams, or a parent planning to support a student through school—in two years or in twenty—this book is your guide on the path to a better education, which will then lead on toward a brighter future and an enriched quality of life.

Chapter 1

Prepare Yourself for College Costs

Have you ever heard the saying, "When you fail to plan, you should plan to fail"? This home wisdom holds especially true when you're choosing ways to pay for college. If you want to be ready for the elevated costs of college, then you'd better know what you're in for and be prepared. Taking action before you go to college is the way to avoid what could otherwise become a serious cash strain. College is a time when your focus should be on academics, not on how to pay for your education.

Get Ready in Advance

It's true. If you're a student, those hard-earned dollars from your part-time job at the local drive-through would be a heck of a lot more fun to spend now, while you're still in high school, on your growing CD collection, movie library, or new and stylish designer labels. If you are a parent, however, you likely find yourself wishing that your student would save some of that cash for college. Don't worry! Your student will realize the importance of saving—the realization might just happen a little later than you would like.

Whether you have many years ahead to build a savings account or only a few, it's worth putting something away. Even a modest amount of savings can be helpful, and not just for paying tuition. A little smart saving can prepare students to pay for some of the more costly items they will need in college, such as a personal computer and pricey textbooks. As little as a few years of sensible saving can also help in paying for tuition (at least for the first year) or could reduce the amount the student or parents have to take out in educational loans.

The federal government makes the assumption that parents will contribute to a student's education. However, prospective students should never assume parents already have a solid plan to pay for college. Corporations are laying off workers and trimming salaries. Money saved for college may end up going to pay the bills, leaving it up to the student to pay his or her way through school.

How Much Can Your Parents Contribute?

This section is primarily for high school grads, soon-to-be grads, and recently enrolled college students in their early twenties. If you are a parent or a nontraditional student (that is, one without family members to help support your further education), you may want to skip to the next section. If you are a younger student hoping to get some financial support from your parents or other relatives, please read on.

Approaching a Parent About Paying for College

A little common-sense preparation can go a long way with your parents, especially if you hope to convince them that it's a good idea to help out with your college tuition. Your parents will be much more inclined to help if you can demonstrate that you are serious—that is, if you're willing to invest some of your *own* money into your education. (By the way, putting half of last week's paycheck into a savings account is not going to cut it.)

These days, many parents are unwilling to risk wasting thousands of dollars in tuition when so many students are partying their way through their college years, finally getting expelled, flunking out, or just plain dropping out when they run out of functional brain cells. By diligently saving your own money with the goal of putting the funds toward college, you will help put your parents' minds at ease. You will let them know that you have the drive to succeed, and you want to go to college so that you can fight to achieve—not just fight for your right to party.

Become a Savings Account Advocate

One or both of your parents might be inclined to open an educational savings account for you, or they may have done so already. If you know for a fact that they have not started saving, now is the time to approach them about opening a college savings account. However, you will have better luck in persuading them to do so if you have a little firepower—in other words, knowledge. Shock them by showing your familiarity with college expenses, rising tuition, and the value of saving. This means your best bet is to keep on reading before you go running into the other room and beg them to start a savings account like you're a two-year-old in a toy store.

Ways for Parents to Save

There are many different types of educational savings accounts to choose from. Some even come with tax benefits and incentives, such as the Coverdell education savings account (ESA) or a qualified tuition program (QTP, also known as a Section 529 plan). Coverdell ESAs used to be called education IRAs. This is an attractive savings plan for families in higher tax brackets. Section 529 plans are somewhat similar to the 401(k) retirement plans so common in business today. The only difference between the two is their goals. Rather than a means of funding retirement, a Section 529 plan is meant to fund a college education. You'll find more information on the Section 529 plan, or the QTP, in the next section; both the Coverdell ESA and the Section 529 plan are discussed in more detail in Chapter 10.

QTPs: Not for Cleaning Out Your Ears!

Most states now have qualified tuition programs (QTPs, or Section 529 plans). Generally, money saved in any individual state's plan is available for use nationwide at any accredited institution of higher learning. Section 529 plans are currently a very popular method of paying for college.

If you are a parent or a nontraditional student, one advantage to the Section 529 plan is that it counts among your assets. You are at little risk of taking a loss with this type of investment, no matter how little you may be able to gain.

What are the benefits to a Section 529 plan? You will learn more about these later, in Chapter 10, but if you are a student, there's one thing you should know right now. A big benefits of having one of these plans is that they are considered among the assets of the account holder (not as a resource of the student/beneficiary) and the beneficiary can be changed at any time, as is necessary. This means that if your big brother decides not to attend college after all, your parents can assign a different beneficiary to the plan—you!

Why is this important? It's a great thing for you to point out when presenting this option to your parents, especially if you have a younger sibling. Simply put, this minimizes their risk for taking a loss if you mess up. You can tell them, "Look, if I end up not getting accepted, or if I go to school and just completely drop the ball, you can always just change the beneficiary over to [insert younger sibling name here] and [he/she] can use it when it comes time for [him/her] to go to school."

The Rising Cost of College Tuition

In the academic year 1999–2000, the average cost for two full-time semesters at a community college, including tuition and fees, was approximately $1,625. At public four-year institutions (which approximately 80 percent of all students attend) the average cost per year was about $3,350—and that was for resident students at in-state schools only. The cost of attending a private institution ran to more than $15,000.

During the 1999–2000 school year, more than half of all undergraduate-level college students attended schools with tuition and fees of less than $4,000 per year. Only 7 percent of undergraduate students that year attended private institutions with fees of $20,000 or more.

Current Tuition Cost Increases

In the 2003–2004 academic year, the collective costs of fees and tuition have gone even further through the roof. Attendance at a four-year public university cost the average college student around $4,700, a jump of more than 14 percent from the previous year. Attending a private institution ran just shy of $20,000, an increase of more than 5 percent.

Not quite a third of all students at four-year colleges in 2003–2004 year paid less than $4,000 for their tuition and fees. About 70 percent of college students at four-year colleges during the same time paid less than $8,000 in academic tuition and fee costs. Only 8 percent of all college students went to institutions where the collective costs totaled a staggering $24,000 or more. This amounts to a substantial financial investment—whether the burden falls on parents who plan to pay their children's way through college or students who plan to pay their own way.

Don't Forget About Room and Board

You will find this phrase repeated again and again as you read through the pages of this book—college students do more than just attend classes at college. Most of the time, students live on campus as well. Some schools even require starting freshmen to live in the dorms. Obviously, this means added expenses. In 2004, the average American college student paid between $340 and $370 more (compared to 2003) for on-campus room and board, depending on the type and location of the college they were attending. At public universities in 2003–2004, students from out of state or out of district paid an extra $3,967 for two-year colleges and $7,046 for four-year colleges, on top of tuition and academic fees. That is a lot of money.

The cost of college tuition rises every year. When you visit colleges, be sure to ask by what percentage their tuition has increased over the past few years. Keep in mind that costs may increase in future years as well. You may be able to qualify for additional financial aid that will help cover some of these increases, but you should still be prepared to pay, just in case.

Difference in Tuition Increases from State to State

Recent tuition and fee increases differ from state to state. The following list shows the percentage by which college tuition and fees increased from the academic year 2001–2002 to 2002–2003.

Increase in annual tuition and fees at public institutions from 2001–2002 to 2002–2003

State	Four-Year Institutions	Two-Year Institutions
National Average	10%	2%
Alabama	7%	7%
Alaska	3%	3%
Arizona	4%	5%
Arkansas	7%	17%
California	5%	No increase
Colorado	8%	6%
Connecticut	9%	8%
Delaware	7%	6%
Florida	5%	3%

(continued)

Increase in annual tuition and fees at public institutions from 2001–2002 to 2002–2003 (continued)

State	Four-Year Institutions	Two-Year Institutions
Georgia	5%	4%
Hawaii	3%	No increase
Idaho	12%	10%
Illinois	9%	7%
Indiana	13%	14%
Iowa	20%	10%
Kansas	7%	7%
Kentucky	11%	6%
Louisiana	4%	6%
Maine	5%	No increase
Maryland	8%	9%
Massachusetts	24%	26%
Michigan	9%	4%
Minnesota	11%	11%
Mississippi	10%	9%
Missouri	20%	10%
Montana	15%	4%
Nebraska	10%	4%
Nevada	3%	3%
New Hampshire	8%	17%
New Jersey	13%	5%
New Mexico	9%	3%
New York	2%	1%
North Carolina	19%	10%
North Dakota	14%	11%
Ohio	17%	8%

(continued)

Increase in annual tuition and fees at public institutions from 2001–2002 to 2002–2003 (continued)

State	Four-Year Institutions	Two-Year Institutions
Oklahoma	9%	6%
Oregon	3%	6%
Pennsylvania	11%	2%
Rhode Island	7%	9%
South Carolina	15%	26%
South Dakota	8%	Not given
Tennessee	8%	7%
Texas	20%	9%
Utah	8%	9%
Vermont	5%	6%
Virginia	9%	13%
Washington	13%	14%
West Virginia	10%	5%
Wisconsin	8%	11%
Wyoming	7%	5%

Figures from the Washington Higher Education Coordination Board; data compiled and completed in January 2003.

Tuition in your state may have increased a lot or a little. Nevertheless, you will note that we're all in the same boat: Tuition increased in all fifty states. And it looks like tuition costs are going to get even higher before they start to get better.

Is It Worth the Price of Admission?

At this point you may be asking yourself if the high cost of tuition is really worth it. Absolutely! Statistics show that more often than not, money spent for a college education is money well spent. On average, you can expect your annual salary to be about $18,000 greater compared to what you would make if you only had a high school diploma. Over a lifetime, a bachelor's degree (or a master's and/or doctorate) is worth more than $1,000,000 more than you could expect to earn if your education stops after high school. This difference grows even bigger if you have earned a degree in a high-tech or computer-related field.

How much is a college degree worth to graduates once they get out in the working world?
According to statistics from the U.S. Census Bureau, Americans with a bachelor's degree earn 60 percent more, on average, than Americans with high school diplomas.

Preparation Is More Than Saving Money

There is more than one way to plan ahead. Whether you're the one headed off to school yourself or you're financially supporting someone who is, you should have more than one plan for paying for this education. Scholarships are not always set in stone, and it will behoove you to have a contingency plan if a worst-case scenario suddenly goes from a hypothetical possibility to an actual situation. In the years before they graduate from high school, students can take a number of preparatory actions that will help them take advantage of all kinds of financial aid possibilities.

High school students, this section is for you, so pay close attention. Parents, you might also want to look at the following information for a better understanding of how to encourage your student.

Use High School to Prepare for College

Prospective college students must be ready to convince admissions officers that they are worthy of being granted admission and that they are prepared to handle the rigors of a college education. Aside from an in-person interview, students demonstrate their readiness primarily through their high school transcripts and scores on standardized aptitude tests like the PSAT (usually taken as a kind of practice for the SAT), the SAT, or the ACT. In order to make your transcript as impressive as is possible, you will need to stretch yourself academically.

However, you should also be careful not to stretch yourself too far. Don't enroll in classes that are so difficult your grade point average suffers as a result. You (and your parents) should be aware of your limitations and set realistic goals. Strive to meet those goals—or even surpass them—but stay within the realm of reason.

A note to parents: You should also be aware of the difference between realistic expectations and pushing too hard. Avoid letting the need for an excellent transcript cloud your good judgment. While it is important to encourage and support your children, you must also be aware of how far is too far.

Take Appropriate College Preparatory Courses

Many colleges, especially those with high admissions standards, prefer to admit students who have taken courses in particular subject areas. For instance, some colleges prefer their students to have taken challenging science and math courses, extending well beyond general math and algebra, while they are still in high school. Basic computer skills have become crucial. Some schools also prefer that students have at least three years of study in one or more foreign languages.

Your guidance counselor can help you figure out what high school courses are required or preferred by the types of colleges where you want to be accepted. If you are interested in a specific type of higher education (a certain major, geographic location, or size of school), whether at a state university, junior college, or vocational school, you may want to contact some of these schools and ask about their individual admissions requirements.

Advanced Placement Courses

Many high schools offer advanced placement (AP) courses and student entrance/course placement tests (sometimes called "leap" exams).

Advanced placement classes are taught at the college level in about fifteen different subjects. Taking these classes during high school or before college is a good way to prepare for college-level work. Students who have taken AP courses have shown themselves to be more prepared for the challenges of college, and admissions administrators have begun to notice this trend.

Besides being good preparation, AP classes can actually earn you college credits. Like any other classes, AP classes are graded. In addition, however, AP students take a standardized AP exam at the end of the year. Exams are scored from 1 to 5, with 5 being a perfect score. At most colleges, an AP score of 3 or higher earns you college credit for the introductory course in that subject. Instead of being required to spend your tuition dollars on the low-level class, you get the credit and are allowed to enroll in a course at the next level. As you can imagine, doing well in your AP classes—and the exams—could mean saving a lot in college costs.

This policy does not hold true at all colleges or for all majors within a given school. Be sure to write to the admissions office at the colleges you're interested in to find out whether they give credit for an AP exam grade over 3. Request a copy of the colleges' different AP policies (in writing—not everyone who answers a phone at a college office knows all policies inside and out). If you have a copy of the college's catalog, check there first to see if it lists the school's policy on AP credit.

If you are a high school student, you can ask your guidance counselor or principal whether your school offers AP courses. If not, you may want to suggest or ask that they consider offering AP courses in the near future. You may even want to bring this book along with you as supporting evidence for your argument. (Parents, feel free to contact the principal or guidance office yourself if you have questions or concerns about the availability of AP courses at your child's school.)

AP courses won't always reduce the number of courses required for your major, but they may cut down on the number of general courses you're required to take. This could help you graduate on time, so you do not have to pay for an extra semester or two. It could also give you more flexibility to take electives for a minor or even a double major.

Courses for the Technically Inclined

If you plan to pursue a technical career at a community, junior, or technical/vocational college, you should supplement or substitute some of your high school fine-arts electives with vocational or technical courses in your field of interest. Many technical fields, such as computer science, require that students have taken advanced math and science courses. Parents should help keep an eye out for more advanced technology courses available during their students' last two years of high school. If you are lucky, these options are available at your high school. If you cannot find the courses you want through your high school, consider community organizations and colleges. Some organizations offer technology classes at very low costs. Your local community or junior college may even have specific sections of courses that are open to local high school students.

Get Involved

Colleges are not just looking for a high GPA these days. While a 4.0 might grease the wheels a bit when a student's scholarship application is being considered, today's colleges also want their students to be well-rounded individuals. Involvement in school activities and in the community can sometimes outweigh even a flawed GPA—and in their absence, even a perfect GPA may fail to shine. For example, a 4.0 student who does nothing but study may lose out on a scholarship (or even admission) to a 3.0 student who is a lacrosse player and avid fencer who volunteers weekends at the local food bank, is a member of the chess club, and holds an officer position in student government.

Advice for Athletes

If you are an athlete, find out when and where the college coaches are going to be seeking out new talent, and try to get yourself to those places. You may be a top-notch athlete, but let's face it—if the college coaches don't know you're out there, let alone know anything about you, you're not going to be the one they recruit.

Every sport has its own special premier events where young talent is showcased. For example, many college volleyball coaches like to do their scouting at volleyball club tournaments all across the country. Getting involved with a club team that actively competes in tournaments can help get you exposure. Do a little research and learn how, when, and where those events for your sport are being held, then find out what you must do to compete in them. Ask one of your high school coaches, contact players you may know who have already been recruited, or search the Internet for any potential athletic events, conferences, or scholarship opportunities.

Remember, even if your high school doesn't offer your favorite sport, the college you hope to attend probably does. For example, few high schools have fencing teams. However, many colleges have them, if not for NCAA competition then at least for recreation. Finding a way to stay involved in your favorite sport may help you get into a college and even win an athletic scholarship.

Alternative Extracurricular Activities

Playing on one of your school's athletic teams is a good way of getting more involved at school—it's certainly a popular one. But there are a number of other ways to participate, not only in school but in community activities as well. If you're a student with no interest in participating on an athletic team, you have plenty of other activity options. Take a look at your strengths, interests, and hobbies. You will probably find a good extracurricular activity—one you can add to your resume—among them.

Parents should actively support and encourage their student to improve and participate in his or her arenas of interest. Keep in mind that any extracurricular activity, regardless of whether it is provided by the student's school, could be a valuable asset for inclusion on an academic resume.

Here are some possibilities to consider:

- Playing a musical instrument (whether in the school band or on your own)
- Performing in theater productions (with your school drama club, community organizations, or a more individual performance, like

reciting your favorite poetry at the local bookstore's open mike night)
- Participating in the Boy Scouts, Girl Scouts, Junior ROTC, Naval Sea Cadet Corps, Campfire, Big Brother/Big Sister, or other constructive youth programs
- Drawing, painting, sculpting, or any other art form
- Dancing, as in ballet, jazz, tap, swing, ballroom competition, native dance, or interpretive dance (does not include spending Friday nights at your local dance club)
- Volunteering (for instance, at a food bank, church, or nonprofit agency)

Participate in any of the above-mentioned activities and you not only increase your chances for acceptance during the admissions application process—you could also tip the odds in favor of being granted extra scholarship opportunities and benefits upon acceptance. Depending on the level and type of your involvement, you can create impressive activities portfolios or even videos of your scholastic achievements and extracurricular performances to accompany your college admissions applications.

Chapter 2

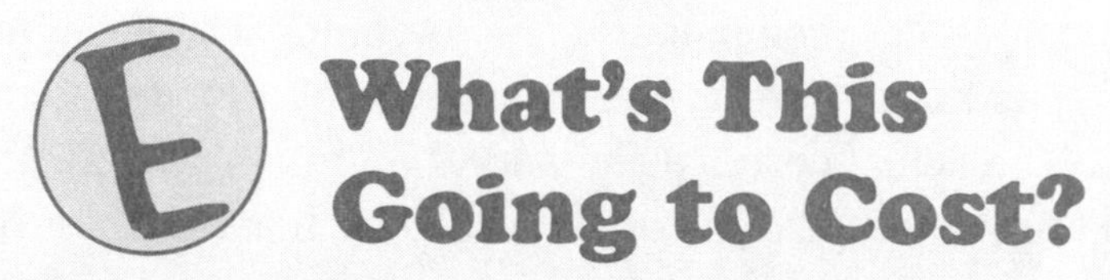

What's This Going to Cost?

In Chapter 1, you learned something about what to expect from tuition costs. When you estimate the total price tag for college expenses, however, it is necessary to understand that tuition costs are only a portion of the total you will actually end up paying. Remember, a college student does not just attend classes. He or she needs a place to live, food to eat, and a way to get around. And that's just the beginning of expenses beyond tuition. Be sure you know what these costs are and that you're prepared for them.

More Than Just Tuition

First of all, you must understand the difference between the "comprehensive fees" at the institution in question and the total "cost of attendance." Comprehensive fees include things that the school will actually include on your bill. Most of the time, these fees include standard college basics such as tuition, mandatory fees (computing access fee, student activities fee, and so on), on-campus housing (residence hall or dormitory), and the dining-hall meal plan. The actual cost of attendance, on the other hand, includes the total for all estimated college costs. Calculating this total cost of attendance sets the limit on what you will be able to receive in financial aid from the school you plan to attend. (You will learn much more about financial aid in Chapter 5.)

Every year, or even every quarter, college financial aid officers consider various elements to estimate the total cost of attendance at their institutions. This could be considered as the average student's budget. Factors that are considered often include the following:

- Tuition and fees
- Room-and-board expenses
- Textbooks, supplies, and personal expenses
- Transportation (gas, public transit, and so on)
- Dependent-care expenses
- Disability-related expenses
- Study-abroad expenses
- Employment-related expenses related to co-op educational programs
- Student loan fees

Take note that not all schools include the same costs in their calculations. University administrators are often required to set reasonable cost boundaries when determining these budget components. They are not, however, under any obligation to include all the above-mentioned categories when calculating their institution's official total cost of attendance.

You may be able to reduce some of your college expenses, such as meal plans or housing. Lower-cost meal plans are sometimes available, and discounts on housing costs may be a possibility if you volunteer to have an extra roommate or agree to take a smaller-than-average room. If you live close enough to campus, consider commuting as a way to eliminate housing costs entirely.

The important thing to remember is that one institution's total may include the costs of study-abroad expenses, for instance, while another institution may exclude them. At an institution with very few older or returning students, administrators probably won't include dependent-care expenses in their total cost of attendance, nor will they likely have any co-op educational programs. Keep in mind that these budget items are calculated for the average student's cost of attendance. You may spend more or less than the totals determined by the standard budgeted amounts.

Comparing Schools By Cost

Because schools don't always include the same items in their calculations of total attendance costs, you should be careful to make an "apples-to-apples" comparison when you are ready to evaluate the costs of different institutions. In other words, match them up element for element, not just cost for cost. If you simply compare different schools in terms of their total estimated cost of attendance, you are assuming that textbook prices, supply costs, and personal expenses are the same, regardless of which schools are being compared—and this is not always the case. Some things simply cost more at different schools or in different areas of the country.

You will also need to make your own adjustments to an institution's budgeted amounts according to your individual situation. If you live on the West Coast and are considering a number of different colleges, some in California and some on the other side of the country, your actual transportation costs will vary greatly depending on the school's distance from home.

Just an Estimate, Please

For a rough estimate of cost comparison, it is okay to compare totals rather than itemize everything specifically. If you feel that you must compare totals, however, be sure that you're consistent. Compare one school's comprehensive fees to the other's, or examine total costs of attendance, but don't mix up the two. If you compare comprehensive fees at NYU to the total cost of attendance at Berkeley, for example, you are going to end up with confusing and misleading results.

Don't Be Scared Off by High Costs!

Neither parents nor students should rule out any institution simply because it has a high cost of attendance. This is very important to keep in mind! Financial aid programs are designed to make the dream of college a reality—even when you dream big. The better prepared for college the student is, and the more the family learns about preparing for and paying the costs, the more opportunities and options will become available at any institution.

Comparing financial aid packages from different schools can be very confusing. Similar types of aid can go under different names at different schools. It will be helpful if you simply categorize each type of aid as a scholarship or grant, a loan, or a work obligation. Then compare the amounts in each of these categories.

The amount of financial aid a student receives can vary tremendously from one institution to the next. Therefore, financial concerns should not really come into play until the student is ready to make that final college choice. For example, state universities usually have much lower comprehensive fees than private institutions. After you calculate the value of scholarships and/or grants you may be awarded at that school, you might find that the private school's net cost is lower than the net cost of a state institution, even though the cost of attendance is much higher.

Cost of Living

Even after running all the numbers, you shouldn't consider your calculation of the cost of attending a particular school to be set in stone. Two students attending the same institution may end up with very different actual costs of attendance. Why? Because depending on a number of factors, the cost of living can vary from person to person. For instance, a student's eating habits may be affected by a wide range of factors, like personal preference, health concerns, religion, the student's accustomed standard of living, and even the student's size and appetite. Schools may charge higher tuition for out-of-state students, and students who live on campus may have different costs of attendance than students who choose to live off campus. Remember, the money that a student must actually spend is not necessarily factored into an institution's official cost of attendance, so you need to make these calculations on your own.

Personal Cost-of-Living Factors

What specific aspects of your lifestyle will affect your wallet when you go off to college? Consider the following examples, and then think carefully about your own personal situation.

If you're an Orthodox Jew, you will only be able to eat food that is kosher. Unless your university has a dining hall dedicated to making dishes that meet kosher dietary requirements, you will probably have to spend money out-of-pocket in order to eat meals in accordance with religious doctrine.

You may be used to getting your hair cut or styled every week, or maybe every other week. While living at home, your parents probably paid this expense. At college, however, you will need to either cut down on the frequency of your hair appointments or allot money for this extra expense.

FACT

Personal choices may be more or less expensive than the estimated costs. The particular meal plan a student chooses, for example, could end up being more or less expensive than the budgeted amount. (Still, you won't get more financial aid simply because you prefer to eat more than the average student.)

"Consumable" Cost of Living

Many of the things college students spend money on are classified as consumables. The "consumables" category includes things like convenience foods, along with other quick-and-easy items commonly found in grocery and drug stores. At the Economic Research Institute's Web site (*www.eri eri.com*), you can use a student cost-of-living calculator that lets you compare any school location's estimated cost of consumables to the national average. After you choose the city where your university or college of choice is located, the calculator will provide you with a "consumable" percentage of the national average. This "consumable" percentage is based upon the assumptions that you are employed and earning at least the minimum wage, are sharing your apartment with roommates, and are paying at least minimum federal and state taxes.

The impact of consumables upon living expenses varies with each student's level of earnings. For example, your consumable expenses may account for just 20 percent of your income, while your roommate and best friend spends a whopping 50 percent. Cost of living depends heavily on the kind of expenditure decisions you make, such as the size and type of your residence, as well as on expenses like income taxes, cost of services, transportation costs, and other miscellaneous items.

Common Non-Tuition Expenses

There are three general expenses not related to tuition that you should definitely keep in mind as you estimate your cost of living will be while at college.

Transportation

If you do not plan to live in the on-campus dormitory—or at least within walking distance of your campus—plan on adding a minimum of $75 a month to your living expenses. This figure will vary. For instance, will you take public transportation or keep your own car (with associated insurance, parking, gas, and maintenance fees)? Be sure to take all costs into account—bus pass or on-campus parking permit—and figure on contingencies like whether you drive yourself or make car pool arrangements.

Books and Supplies

You should plan to spend about $1,000 on textbooks and general supplies each year. If you plan to study a specialized, technical subject (math and sciences, for instance), or if you plan to study subjects requiring special materials (film, fine arts), you may want to allot additional funds for the purchase of specialized textbooks as well as course-specific instruments and supplies.

Board and Lodging

Depending on your choice of meal plan and the availability of rooms on campus, costs for room and board can range as high as $4,500 to $8,000 or more per year. If you plan to live in the dorm, or even in an apartment, you should plan to spend approximately $135 per week to keep a roof over your head and food in your stomach.

Most colleges and universities keep a housing registry, which lists the various kinds of living accommodations that are available in the area. For specific information, consult a counselor at your institution's residential life office.

How Much for Those Textbooks?

In 1998, the national average cost for a college textbook was $61.50. This represented an increase of $4 from the previous year, according to the National Association of College Stores. In recent years, textbook costs have grown much higher. In fact, prices have gone up so much that they have raised national attention—to the point that consumers have even called for the government to investigate!

Survey of Textbook Costs

To find out how much students really spend on textbooks, the California Student Public Interest Research Group (CALPIRG), Oregon Student Public Interest Research Group (OSPIRG), and the OSPIRG Foundation conducted a survey. They looked at the most widely required college textbooks during the fall semester of 2003 at ten public colleges and state universities in both California and Oregon. More than 150 faculty members and more than 500 students were interviewed about the cost of textbooks and individual purchasing preferences. The main findings of the survey were are follows:

- College students spent an average of $898 per year on both new and used textbooks in 2003–2004. This represents nearly 20 percent of the average tuition and fees for in-state students at public four-year colleges nationwide. (An earlier survey at the same schools found that in 1996–1997, the average cost of textbooks was $642.)
- Roughly 50 percent of college-level textbooks now come in bundled packages or have been shrink-wrapped with additional materials (such as interactive CD-ROMs or supplemental workbooks). Students are often not given the option of buying these textbooks without the additional materials, even if they do not plan or need to use them.
- In only one instance was a textbook available in both bundled and unbundled (textbook only) packages. The bundled version cost more than two times as much as the unbundled version of the same college textbook.
- Approximately 65 percent of professors and college instructors said they rarely made use of the bundled packages' extra materials in their college courses.
- According to 76 percent of professors and instructors, new editions of textbooks were "never" to "half the time" justified. A full 40 percent of professors and instructors reported that the new college textbook editions were "rarely" to "never" justified.
- New college textbooks cost an average of $102. This is 58 percent more expensive than the average price of used textbooks, which is close to $65.
- Of college students who specifically wanted used textbooks, 59 percent were unable to find even one used textbook for their entire schedule of classes.

FACT

The amount of money students spend on textbooks can vary greatly, depending on the type of class (with science books tending to cost more than other disciplines), the number of books each professor requires, and whether the student can find any used copies.

Textbook Costs in Politics

Even in politics, the rising prices of college textbooks have become a heated issue of debate. Representative David Wu of Oregon recently introduced a bill in the U.S. House of Representatives calling for an investigation into the pricing policies of some of the nation's foremost publishers of college textbooks. The bill, introduced on November 11, 2003, was turned over to the House Committee on Education and the Workforce, of which Wu is a member.

The push for an investigation into the publishing industry's pricing policies came less than a month after a *New York Times* front-page article that was printed on October 21, 2003. The article exposed the incredibly high textbook prices that American college students have been forced to pay.

Other recent studies have revealed that U.S. college bookstores are forced to sell textbooks at double the price they sell for overseas, and that American college bookstores are often forbidden from selling less expensive alternatives to students, such as condensed, course-specific, or paperback editions. Representative Wu confirmed these findings in a public demonstration at Portland State University's bookstore on November 7, 2003.

What Does the New Bill Mean?

The bill Representative Wu introduced soon after his November demonstration assigns this investigation to the federal government's General Accounting Office (GAO). If this bill is passed, it will be the job of the GAO to inspect the situation thoroughly and report its findings back to the House of Representatives within one year.

Although rising college textbook prices are being brought into the open, they remain, nonetheless, as they are—ridiculously high. So be prepared to pay them. (There are some things you can do to save some money, however. For tips, see Chapter 9.)

The more necessary items you bring with you to college, the less you will have to buy later. It would be wise to make a list of these items and take at least a shopping day or two to locate and purchase them in advance.

School Supplies

Keep in mind that you will also be spending money on school supplies. By "school supplies," we mean more than just pencils, pens, paper, and the other usual stuff you geared up with during your high school years. Remember, as a college student, you will be doing more than simply going to classes—you will probably live there as well. So it is important for you to bring the right kind of gear for the job. By doing this, you can save yourself a lot of money in the long run.

Buy Certain Items in Advance

Don't forget—it is almost always easier to find things cheaper in your own hometown than it will be at the on-campus store of a new school. Of course, you will first need to know what to buy. Don't rush around without a plan and start impulse buying, wasting money on a bunch of things you will probably not even need.

For example, the cost of residence hall rooms may include use of a small refrigerator or microwave. Before you go out and purchase these items, find out from the institution's residential life office if these amenities are included or whether you can rent them.

Before you go out and buy any small appliances for your dorm room, be sure the residence hall policy allows for them. You should also check to see whether your roommate has already bought a fridge or microwave that you might be able to share. If you must buy these items, watch the classified ads and buy used if you can.

To give you an idea of the kinds of things you should plan to buy in advance, here are some essential items that most college students will want to have:

- **Shower bucket/tote**—This handy carryall can be rolled or carried from a student's room to the bathroom. (In dorms, students may share a bathroom with quite a few people.) If you leave things sitting unsupervised in a community bathroom, they could get stolen. Or worse, someone you do not know (and do not want to share hygiene products with) will use them.
- **Cheap, nonperishable food items**—We all get hungry sometimes, and the dining hall isn't always open. Peanut butter, macaroni and cheese, and dry cereal are all good to have in a dorm room. They won't go bad and stink up the room. You can also consider drink options like instant coffee, tea bags, hot cocoa mix, or Kool-Aid.
- **Writing materials**—This includes an address book, stationery, spiral notebooks and notebook paper, envelopes (and postage stamps).
- **Stuff to eat/drink with**—Find a cheap plastic bowl, reusable (yet disposable) plate, fork and spoon, large plastic cup, mug for coffee, and a travel mug if you plan to take that coffee to class (spilled coffee in class is a quick way to get on the professor's bad side).
- **Clothes-drying rack**—Dormitory dryers do not always work. Sometimes they work a little too well. Apart from the fact that they do not always perform as you would like, they usually cost money to use. A drying rack can help you save your money and your clothes.
- **Plastic basin**—This can be used as a second sink or just as a dirty dish holder (but definitely not for both purposes simultaneously).
- **Write-on/wipe-off board**—Messages are often unreliable when left in a dorm, and your answering machines won't help if someone stops by your room and you're not around. One of those small dry-erase boards posted on or by your dorm room door is a great way for your friends to leave messages when you're out of the room.
- **Laundry bag or basket**—You'll need one of these to carry your laundry to and from the laundry room. Remember, laundry baskets work better if you actually fold the laundry once it's done.

- **Alarm clock**—Be sure you buy one with a snooze button. As a college student, you don't have the luxury of mumbling "Just five more minutes, Mom."
- **"Plasti-tac" putty**—This stuff is great for hanging things on your dorm room walls. Colleges usually do not allow tape or nails to be used for hanging posters, pictures, plaques, and so on. If you plan to get an off-campus apartment, it will be easier to get your security deposit back if you haven't put a lot of holes in the walls.
- **Flashlight and extra batteries**—Blackouts can happen.
- **Mini medicine cabinet**—Include a small box of aspirin, cold/flu medicine, band-aids, and so on. Moms feel better knowing their students have these items with them.

These things will be cheapest at your local thrift store or the dollar store—you're not looking for quality here, as the odds are good that you won't have any of them for very long. In fact, you shouldn't bring anything with you to college that you are not willing to have lost, stolen, broken, warped, or otherwise ruined and tossed out.

Be Resourceful

As a student, you should take advantage of the opportunities available on campus for getting "free" school supplies. You can often get free pencils and pens from clubs, organizations, student government officers, and other groups who are recruiting, campaigning, or just trying to get publicity. There are also places where you can use supplies without having to buy them yourself. Libraries often have a stapler, hole punch, and other such items that you can drop by and use. (Students should remember to *use* these items, not *steal* them).

Other Possible Incidental Expenses

Additional expenses aside from tuition that may not be included in the cost of attendance are music lesson fees, course lab and other special class fees, computer-related expenses, and pizza money. (The campus cafeteria will not be open late at night when you unexpectedly get the munchies.)

It is tempting to join the crowd when your friends are going out to eat, but for the student on a budget, dining out regularly is costly. Put aside a small amount of money each week so that you can participate in outings without going broke.

In addition to the costs of basic room and board, off-campus lodging, and tuition, you must also consider incidental expenses when estimating the total cost for a year of attendance at a university or college. The general range of incidental expenses commonly runs between $1,800 and $2,000 a year. This covers items we've already discussed, such as books and supplies, as well as personal expenses for laundry, cleaning, recreation, and minor clothing replacements. You should also budget premiums for accident and health insurance, which is highly recommended.

Remember that incidental expenses for a college education will vary according to your tastes and the activities you participate in. Costs for items such as laundry, personal needs, and entertainment will vary according to individual preferences. If you take courses in graphic arts, painting, sculpting, and the like, the cost of your course supplies may be somewhat higher. Students who plan to join fraternities, sororities, honor societies, or certain student groups will have to factor in dues, social events, honor banquets, and other possible incidentals that come with membership.

Chapter 3

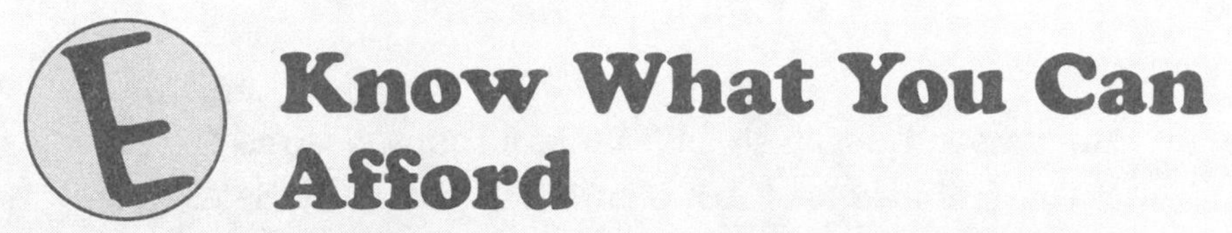

Know What You Can Afford

Your financial boundaries are yours and yours alone. They determine what portion of your current cash flow you can afford to put toward college. This chapter explains what these boundaries are, how to identify them, and how to stay inside them. But that's not the end of the line—once you know your current financial boundaries, you have to decide whether you want to remain within their limits or whether you are willing to stretch a little and invest more in your future.

Understanding Financial Boundaries

The process of understanding your financial boundaries involves three essential steps: figuring out what financial boundaries are (and what they are not), learning how to identify your own, and knowing how to stay within them. Let's start with step one.

FACT

Students and parents shouldn't rule out applying to certain schools just because of their total cost of attendance. Even students of very modest financial means can afford to attend costly Ivy League institutions if they receive enough financial aid. However, they need to be prepared by cultivating an understanding of their financial boundaries.

As a parent, it is important that you understand your financial boundaries. If you know what you can afford, you and your student will be able to choose a school realistically. Everyone will only become frustrated if you don't realize your boundaries until after the student has his or her heart set on a certain college. What will you do when your student gains admission only to find that you are uninformed or unprepared to make up for the costs that are outside your immediate financial boundaries?

Financial boundaries are not meant to discourage you or to sway your confidence in your ability to pay for a college education. This is simply a way for you to get a ballpark idea of what you have as a base for paying for college. Knowing your boundaries gives you a chance to take a hard, realistic look at your financial situation so you can figure out what you need in order to fund your journey to a higher education.

What Are Financial Boundaries?

Roughly speaking, financial boundaries are the limits of your finances. They give you a clear understanding of what you can and cannot afford. This information can help you plan ahead, allowing you to determine your needs by defining what you already have. This is also a good way to get an early heads-up about whether you need or qualify for certain kinds of financial aid.

Especially in these tough economic times, many parents and students are living from month to month or from paycheck to paycheck, with no substantial savings worth speaking of. Though a month-to-month budget is not the ideal situation, and certainly not one that most people would choose, it does not put college out of reach.

Can Boundaries Keep You from College?

Going to college should never be a matter of "if." Decide, right from the start, that you *are* going to go to college. If you go into this with a negative mindset, your chances of success are going to be slim. Questions are fine, but instead of "Am I going?" the questions you should ask are "How much?" "When?" "What kind?" and "Where?" In other words, spend time asking yourself the following helpful questions:

- *How much* money do you and your family have, in savings or otherwise?
- *When* do you expect to have more?
- *What kind* of school do you wish to attend?
- *Where* in the family, or elsewhere, can you go for help? (This includes loans and other financial aid.)

Students and parents should discuss the kinds of financial aid the student is eligible for, know the source of each type of aid, and understand any obligations associated with that assistance. When parents and students act as a team in this regard, they are able to recognize that a college degree truly is an investment in time and money. Then they appreciate the sacrifices and contributions each are making toward the education.

Calculating Financial Boundaries

By following three simple steps, you will be able to create a budget-based definition of your financial boundaries. These steps include figuring out your income, taking a look at the past, and making your calculations. Remember that these steps should be based upon more than just parental income and savings. The student's salary, student loans, and any other source of income should also be included. Establishing a rough figure of your budget-based boundaries is the first step to taking control of your finances.

Know Where Your Money Comes From

Begin by making a complete list of all sources of income. Be sure to include full-time wages, pending contract jobs (without counting any chickens before they hatch), and student loans. If they apply to your situation, even alimony and child support can be figured into this amount. This list should reflect your net income, that is, your income after taxes. When in doubt, low-ball yourself. It is always better to work from a low estimate than to overshoot and come up short.

Take a Look Back

You know the saying, "Never look back?" Well, for this second step, you have no choice. Get ready to examine your financial situation of the last few years. Don't do this task by memory—you need accurate figures. So get out all the papers you have (such as checkbook registers, credit card statements, receipts, and bills). The goal is to list all your expenses (that is, expenditures that you can't deduct on your income tax return) and come up with a month-to-month average.

Begin with your fixed expenses. These are the bills you pay each month, such as the rent or mortgage, car payments, or payments on another kind of loan. Fixed expenses, in other words, are those whose payment amounts stay the same from one month to the next. (Things such as electricity or water bills do not figure into this part—hold onto those for later.) Some fixed expenses are less frequent—that is, you pay these bills periodically, perhaps every three months or every year. This category includes vehicle registration and inspection, life insurance premiums, car insurance, and so on. Figure these items into your list by dividing the yearly totals by twelve and then adding the result into your monthly calculations.

Next, it is time to tally up your variable expenses. These are the expenditures that change from one month to the next, including phone or utility bills, gas, groceries, clothes, day care, home maintenance, and any substantial entertainment expenses (say, any time that you spent more than $25 in a month). Be honest with yourself. Add up your receipts, and if you do not have them, overestimate. Do not forget to add in a little extra to account for "walking around money," those nickels and dimes that seem to disappear into some kind of fiscal oblivion. Once you have accounted for all your variable expenses, you can proceed in one of two ways. You can add up all expenditures for the year and divide the total by twelve, or you can add up expenditures in any twelve individual months and take their average. Either way, the result will be a good representation of your variable monthly expenses.

Take your time, and make sure you've gotten financial aid information from all your schools of choice before you make your final decision. Remember, your actual net cost can vary greatly from one place to another, and you do not want to find out too late that you could have gone to a better school for the same money (or less).

It's Math Time

You can now add the monthly totals of your fixed expenses and your variable expenses to come up with an estimate of your total monthly expenditures. Subtract this expenditure total from your total income. The result will give you a basic, budget-based estimate of your financial boundaries. If this final number is negative (less than zero), don't panic! You may just need to cut down on some of your variable expenses. With a little penny-pinching creativity, you might be able to cut down in some areas considerably (such as entertainment), without too much difficulty.

Stay Within Your Financial Boundaries

Now that you have defined and identified your personal financial boundaries, you need to decide on a school that is within your grasp by using these boundaries as a guide—not as a restriction. As you have already learned, just because a school is too pricey right now doesn't mean that it always will be. Financial boundaries need to be identified so you have a fairly accurate idea of how much you can pay toward your college education from month to month. If you choose to extend yourself beyond your boundaries, you must know that you are taking on some element of risk. At the same time, you can be relatively assured that your income after graduation will be sufficient to pay back any additional monthly amounts.

Extra-Wide Boundaries Mean Extra Savings

Here's an alert for anyone with at least a year to save money for college: Your budget-based boundary amount can lead to savings! Once you have a solid understanding of your income and expenditures, you have more control over your money and the way you spend it. It is recommended that you set aside no less than 5 percent of your net income for college savings.

Unfortunately, 5 percent of one person's income is not going to be the same as 5 percent of someone else's income. For example, for someone who has an income of $30,000 a year, savings of 5 percent will add up to $1,500 a year. For someone who makes $50,000, however, this total will be $2,500. Your financial boundaries will have a large impact on what you are able to save. Knowing your numbers will help you figure out how much you can save and keep you from either not saving enough or going overboard.

Over a five-year period, the person earning $30,000 a year will have saved around $7,500 (given that the person saved consistently, without spending any funds, and that savings earned no interest). In the same time, the person earning $50,000 will rack up $12,500. That extra $1,000 a year could make a big difference in the long run.

Don't assume that you make too much money to qualify for financial aid. It won't hurt you (too much) to research your options and fill out a few forms. You might be surprised to find out what you do qualify for!

If you define your financial boundaries now, it will be easier to see what a huge difference even an extra $1,000 a year can make to your overall savings. This in turn may help you to realize possibilities you have yet to think of. An extra $1,000 a year is not too difficult to earn. Knowing you need it may help motivate you to find ways of earning extra money and earmarking it for your college savings.

In fact, one savings account may not be enough. It is common for a savings account to suddenly become an emergency account during times of financial trouble—even if those funds are dedicated to college. In order to avoid this, you should set aside an additional 3 percent or so of your net income for a "contingency plan" account. This is money you can dip into, when necessary, so your college savings don't get devoured. With such an account, you will be prepared for extra costs, such as an unexpected car repair or emergency travel. As a result, you will be able to reserve your college savings for their intended purpose.

Giving Your Financial Boundaries a Boost

Financial boundaries are not to be feared, and they should never be perceived as a curse. These boundaries do not condemn you, nor do they confine you in any way, shape, or form. In fact, there are a number of ways to improve or expand the abilities and limits of your financial boundaries. Staying positive is crucial, and the following tips may be just what you need to help you get started making your financial picture better than it ever has been.

Avoid Creating Excessive Debt

Excessive debt? What is that? Well, just ask a majority of the American population. In the United States, debt continues to rise among the average citizen while the amount and frequency of our individual savings have plummeted to a frighteningly low level. We live in a world of immediate gratification, where a plastic card can seemingly give us anything we want, when we want it, without seeing any "actual" money leave our hands.

There is no such thing as "magic credit." Never forget how that money has to be paid back (and then some). If credit cards are a problem for you, turn to Chapter 19 for some helpful advice.

Trim Your Expenses

Reduce the money your family spends on entertainment and other variable expenses by looking for low- to no-cost alternatives. For example, suppose your family traditionally enjoys a weekend movie night. Don't assume you always have to show up at the theater as the sun sets on a Friday or Saturday. There are several other options to consider. For instance, you could do any of the following:

- See a matinee instead of an evening show.
- Go to the dollar theater and see a second-run movie.
- Rent a movie from the video store.
- Check out a movie from your local library.

You don't have to stop having fun; you just need to start thinking—before you do things—about how much money your fun is costing you. Consider cheaper methods of entertainment whenever you can, and eventually you will see significant changes in the tightness of those financial boundaries. Reducing your family's expenses may mean making a few temporary sacrifices to your customary lifestyle or luxuries. However, in the long run you will find that the reward of providing for your college education was well worth the sacrifice.

Here are a few more suggestions for trimming your expenses as much as possible:

- Read magazines at the library instead of subscribing.
- Find car and home insurance with lower premiums/rates.
- Cut down your cable/satellite bill by switching to a smaller plan.
- Learn to do minor home repairs (within reason) instead of hiring pros.

Another thing to watch out for is excessive cell phone usage. Cell phones and those "out-of-plan" minutes are becoming a notorious means of eating up a family's hard-earned money. Keep tabs on all the minutes each member of your family uses—including yourself. Talk too much, or use too many of those newfangled download options (ring tones are especially popular among today's teens) and you'll find yourself with some high, and often very unexpected, expenses when the bill arrives in the mail. It's definitely in your best interest to stay within the allotted minutes on your wireless plan.

If it's just too difficult to stick to your current cell phone plan, it might be wise to consider upgrading so that your bill never exceeds your base monthly charge. A new, bigger plan may only cost you an extra $50 or so a month. However, if every member of your family consistently runs up extra minutes, you're probably already paying hundreds more.

For you homeowners (especially you parents) out there, refinancing your mortgage might be a good way to help expand your financial boundaries. If you can get a significantly lower interest rate, you can open up more available funds to pay for your student's higher education. This is a very valid idea, especially in these times when interest rates are at historic lows.

Find Tax Incentives

You can also find ways to save on your income taxes. No, this book is not advising you to cheat on your taxes! That will only cost you more money in the long run, when the IRS decides to audit you, not to mention that it's against the law. One of the best ways to save on your income taxes is to take advantage of tax incentives, which besides being perfectly legal can be helpful as well.

The Taxpayer Relief Act

As a result of the Taxpayer Relief Act of 1997, the IRS has enacted tax incentives for costs related to higher education. Specifically, the act makes two relevant additions to the tax code: the Hope Scholarship credit and the Lifetime Learning tax credit. The act also added a deduction for student loan interest.

Along with those credits and deductions, the Taxpayer Relief Act of 1997 also made it possible to get tax-free financial aid (or educational assistance) from your employer. Amendments were also made to the provisions that define eligibility for Section 529 plans (or qualified tuition programs, as discussed in Chapter 10).

These provisions have created several new tax benefits for a lot of American families, whether they are saving up for higher education costs, already paying for them, or just repaying student loans. Certain factors determine whether a taxpayer can take advantage of these benefits, such as financial situation, facts, and circumstances. Visit the IRS Web site at *www.irs.gov* for a more detailed review of the requirements for each of these benefits. **(The above information was provided to the public by the Internal Revenue Service's Notice 97-60: Administrative, Procedural, and Miscellaneous Education Tax Incentives.)**

Hope Scholarship Tax Credit

As a taxpayer, you can claim the Hope Scholarship credit for qualified tuition and college-related expenses for every student in your family (that includes you, your spouse, and any dependents). Students must be enrolled with at least a 50-percent course load. They must be in the first two years of higher education and be enrolled in a degree program or one that will earn some other form of nationally recognized vocational/educational credential.

As your income increases over the $40,000 threshold ($80,000 if you are married and filing jointly), the amount you can claim in Hope Scholarship credit will be reduced little by little. If you earn more than $50,000 ($100,000 if married filing jointly), you will no longer be eligible for this credit.

The amount that a taxpayer can claim as Hope Scholarship credit is determined as follows. You may claim 100 percent of the first $1,000 of out-of-pocket expenses for each student's tuition and college-related expenses, plus an additional 50 percent from the second $1,000 of these expenses. Therefore, the maximum amount of Hope Scholarship credit that you can claim in a tax year will equal $1,500 multiplied by the number of students in your family who meet the enrollment criteria.

Taxpayers with modified gross incomes of more than $50,000 ($100,000 if married filing jointly) are ineligible to claim Hope Scholarship tax credit. These limits—both on income and on the amount of expenses that can be claimed—were set to match inflation rates in 2002. They have not yet been modified.

The Lifetime Learning Tax Credit

Whether the student in your family is your spouse, your child, or you yourself, as a taxpayer you may be eligible to claim the Lifetime Learning credit (depending on your income). This credit applies to out-of-pocket tuition payments and other college-related expenses for students enrolled in a recognized institution of higher education. You are entitled to claim up to 20 percent of your first $10,000 in out-of-pocket tuition and college-related expenses, or up to $2,000. Unlike the Hope scholarship credit, these expense limits are not being indexed/adjusted to meet the rate of inflation.

If you claim a Hope Scholarship credit for your daughter, a college student, then your daughter may not apply any of her own out-of-pocket college-related expenses for that year may toward her Lifetime Learning credit. The amount that any taxpayer may claim in Lifetime Learning credit is gradually reduced as gross income increases to more than $40,000 ($80,000 if married filing jointly). If you earn more than $50,000 ($100,000 if married filing jointly), you are no longer eligible to claim this credit. The modified gross income limit will be indexed for inflation, as with the Hope Scholarship credit.

Understanding Tuition—Myth and Reality

We all know what tuition is. However, for someone who has never actually paid it, such as a first-generation college student or a parent whose own college years were funded by a parent or relative, the tuition payment process needs a little explanation. The good news is that tuition payments are a lot more flexible than many people think, and schools are becoming more and more lenient about how and when tuition must be paid.

Do colleges have payment plans?
Yes, most institutions offer a payment plan that lets you divide tuition for the whole academic year into monthly payments. This makes the cost to families much more manageable. Schools usually don't charge any interest, but you might be assessed a minimal service charge.

Many myths surround the process of paying tuition, especially concerning when and how this should happen. Some say it must be paid in full before classes start, while others claim that a student cannot register for classes until all money owed to the school has been paid. According to still other sources, a student will be taken off the roll immediately if the tuition has not been paid. It's a good idea to take a look at these points and figure out what's true and what's not.

Is Tuition Paid Before School Begins?

Yes and no. If you take a look at most schools' formal policies, they state that a student's tuition payments must be current in order for the student to attend class. However, this policy revolves around a loophole. As long as the school receives payment of some kind, it is inconsequential whether the student has actually paid a single dime out of pocket. Loans, even emergency loans, count as forms of tuition payment.

Many colleges now have what they call "emergency" semester loans, which are granted to any student for a single term of attendance. This loan takes the lump sum of the semester's tuition and breaks it down into smaller increments that can be paid out over a period of time. Commonly, there are three pay increments. In other words, if your tuition for a semester is $1,800, you will make three payments of approximately $600 over the span of the semester.

Is a Missed Payment Grounds for Dismissal?

No. These emergency loans may be broken up into increments, but the school does not usually resort to drastic measures if the full portion is not paid by the deadline. Consider the following true example of how tuition payments can work.

A certain student has a total semester tuition cost of $1,800. He pays with an emergency loan, broken up into three $600 increments. These payments are due within the first three months of the semester. However, this student also served in the military, and under the GI Bill he is entitled to a $900 check after each month of completed and verified full-time college attendance. Now, let's say that our student uses half of the $900 to pay his tuition, with the other half going to cover living expenses as well as the cost of textbooks and course supplies. Instead of $600, the amount of his incremental payment, the student only has $450 to put toward his tuition. However, he pays that $450 every month. Aside from the occasional late charge, the school business office does not even bat an eye. As long as a school is receiving some payment, they often let something as small as incomplete payments slide by.

Just because a school is lenient about enforcing its payment deadlines, you should not assume that it ignores them completely. Schools will issue fines and late charges. If you can pay on time, do so. If not, take the fine, and pay when you can. Just remember that you need to keep the balance of your account low enough so that your school won't put a hold on it, which can prevent you from registering or receiving a report card.

It's best not to assume that this example will also hold true at your school. If you're having a problem making your tuition payments on time or in full, you should contact the business office and discuss your options they have. Ask whether partial payments, such as those in the above example, are a possibility. The simple act of going to the business office to discuss your problem—along with your assurance that you fully intend (and will be able) to pay your tuition—can be enough to open some doors. On the other hand, if they do not hear from you, the school's business office has little choice but to assume the worst. Help them out by going to them and discussing your situation face-to-face.

If Next Semester Isn't Paid Up, Can I Register?

There is leeway on registration up to a certain point. Most schools will allow students to register for classes as long as their balance does not exceed a certain amount. At Midwestern State University, for example, a student who owes the school less than $500 is still allowed to register for the next semester. However, if the student's account goes above the $500 ceiling, a "freeze" or "hold" is placed on the account. This prevents the student from registering, receiving certain honors or awards, and sometimes from receiving a report card or even graduating.

FACT

A "freeze" or "hold" can put a real damper on the close of your semester, especially if it keeps you from registering early for the next semester's classes, receiving a student honor that you were eligible for, or even from getting your grades at term's end.

Even though there is some flexibility when it comes to when and how you pay that tuition bill, the fact remains that it must be paid. If you find yourself struggling to make those payments, be sure that you do pay what you are able. Also be sure that you keep your account current (and out of delinquent status) by bringing your balance down under your school's "tuition owed" ceiling before the semester's end.

Chapter 4

In the Beginning, Choices Must Be Made

Before you can start heading in the right direction, it's imperative to have a general idea of where you want to end up. Both students and parents need to think about what makes an ideal school—for starters, you may want to focus on the student's interests and personal strengths. Using those as a springboard, do some research and come up with a list of colleges you're interested in. You can base your choices on institution size, majors offered, or distance from home—whatever is most important to you and/or your student.

Know Your Strengths

The first thing that students and their parents need to do is to start thinking about the student's interests and personal strengths. If you're the kind of student who scores high in language classes such as English or Spanish, and you are active in dance, art, or drama, then schools with good liberal arts programs would be a natural choice for starting out your search for potential colleges. If you get very high grades in mathematics and science classes, and you were good at advanced subjects like calculus, computer programming, and/or physics (classes many high school students never take because they get stuck at the lower levels), then a more technical school that focuses on fields related to math and science would be an excellent choice for you.

Once you have identified the student's strengths, weaknesses, and interests, it is time to start looking. Maybe you already have some schools in mind. Write them down, and start a list of schools to research further. Ask your school guidance counselor for advice on schools that might fit your strengths and interests. You can also go online and search for schools by the program or major you are interested in. Using any search engine, such as Google or Yahoo, type in your search keywords as follows: "college university [name of major] major."

Pay attention to ratings and rankings of colleges and universities, but do not put too much emphasis on them when making your decision. There are other factors, such as campus life, internship options, and activities that each individual student should consider.

Ask for Information—It's Always Free!

The only thing that comes free when it comes to college is information. Schools are more than happy to send prospective students all the information they possibly can—all you have to do is ask. Once you have a list of possible schools, it's time to find out all you can about each and every one of them. All you have to do is request an information packet from the school's admissions office. Even better, many schools now honor e-mail requests for information. Just go to the school's Web site to find out if they offer this option. Remember that the best decision is an informed decision. The information is free, and the schools are happy to give it to you, so there is no excuse for not requesting these useful little packets from all the schools on your list.

Are You Ready to Apply?

Once you have received information from all schools, you may find that some are obvious standouts—they have the program or major you're interested in, a great location, and the kind of campus life you're looking for. If you feel this good about a school, go ahead and start working on an application. (Skip straight ahead to the application advice on the pages that follow to help you get started.)

College visits are a good way of making sure that a school is as wonderful as it sounds in those official brochures you've been reading. If you're still unsure about a school, you might as well wait to apply until you can make a visit. But remember, just because you apply to a certain school does not mean you have to go to there. The sooner you apply, the sooner the school will send you information about the financial aid possibilities they can offer you.

Get Those Applications out Early

If you are a person who likes to start things off already in the lead position, you may want to think about applying for early admission. If you are procrastinator, it's a good idea to get started right now! There are commonly two avenues of attack for people who want to get a jump on things. The first is called early action.

Early action is an admissions decision that binds the university or college to the student applicant, but it does not bind the applicant to the school. What does this mean to you as a student? It means that the school is left with no choice but to let you in when your first semester rolls around. However, you are able to retain your power of choice and may go to college somewhere else should you decide to do so.

The second avenue of attack is called early decision. An early decision admission is a little more restrictive, as it is binding for both the school and the applicant. This means that you and the school have a contractual agreement that you are not only admitted, you will definitely attend.

Make 100-percent sure that you know which schools offer what options before you sign any early admission contract. Also make sure that you are fully aware of the dates for all early paperwork (or other) deadlines.

First Come, First Served?

Even if you don't think early admission is for you, you still have no excuse for unnecessary procrastination. Students and parents should plan to get regular applications to the post office ahead of deadline time. This is the best way of making sure there will be placements available. Didn't expect that one, did you? Well, believe it or not, certain schools operate on a "first come, first serve" basis of admission. This is technically known as a "rolling admission" policy. Instead of waiting for the deadline to pass and evaluating all applications, admissions officers look at each application as it arrives. As students are accepted, spots are assigned in the incoming class. If any of the schools on your list uses this method, it's important to send your applications off as early as you can (as long as you don't drive yourself crazy in the process!).

Visit More Than One School!

Visit as many of the schools you're interested in as you can. If you are a traditional student, the college you attend will most likely become your home away from home for most of the academic year. If all goes as planned, it will continue to be home for the next four years. Think about it like this—would you purchase a house and move in without ever having taken a look at it? Almost anyone would want to at least glance inside. In the same way, you want to make sure that you will be comfortable enough at your school that you can be an efficient student.

If you feel terribly overwhelmed during only be a short visit, you can just imagine how you might feel later—weeks into the semester, after you factor in the stress of classes and homework every day. On the other hand, don't underestimate your adaptation skills, either. (Think back to how intimidating your high school was at the beginning of your freshman year compared to how you see it now.) Just be sure you have an idea what you are getting yourself into. If you fall in love with a school at first sight, you may know it's the one for you; if it's not even close to what was represented in the brochures, you may end up crossing it off your list. This is why it's important to keep your options open and visit as many schools as you can.

FACT

Smaller colleges tend to attract students from the college's immediate geographic region. These candidates are generally well-prepared for college. National liberal arts colleges tend to admit students from wider geographic and social backgrounds who have exceptionally strong academic backgrounds. They emphasize undergraduate education and may or may not offer graduate programs.

Prepare Your Paperwork

Gather your financial aid information (the school needs data for you and your parents), so you will have it together and ready when you need to complete certain financial aid forms. This includes copies of federal tax returns, particularly for the year before the one when you plan to enter college. Necessary papers may also include (but are not limited to) W-2 or W-4 income statements, receipts for cash income, personal savings records, bank account statements, and investment accounts. You may want to call each school's financial aid office to find out what other paperwork they require. You do not want find yourself at the financial aid office with a pile of papers only to be told, "There is another form you forgot. You will have to fill this out and come back later."

Get yourself a file folder (one that can be securely closed with a clasp or tie) and keep your important financial notes, statements, and papers in it. Be meticulous about this—if you take papers out, put them back as soon as you are done with them or if you will not need them for more than an hour. This prevents papers from being lost or accidentally discarded. Mark the folder with a label like "Important Papers!" or "Do Not Throw Away!"

Are You Asking the Right Questions?

Before you go off to make a serious visit to a prospective university or college campus, you should be sure you have completed all the required forms by the set deadlines. During your visit, or even by phone before you go, you should make sure to ask questions such as those found in the following list:

- When is your admissions application deadline?
- What financial aid forms do you require, and what are the deadlines?
- What types of financial aid do you offer to students?
- Is there a separate application for academic scholarships?
- Are any types of financial aid "guaranteed?"
- When can I expect to receive my financial aid package?

Do not rest until all of your questions have been answered to your full satisfaction. Avoid the possibility of "bad-rumor syndrome" or of misinformation by always making an effort to ask the appropriate people the appropriate questions.

Decide by Seeing, Not by Being Told

It is very easy to allow yourself to become distracted by the "glamour and glitter" that many universities put on during visitor tours for prospective students. As far as the school is concerned, there is a good reason to stage this kind of show—they want you to want to go to their school because more students means more money for them. Convincing you means selling the idea of their school to you in very much the same way a door-to-door vacuum cleaner salesman tries to convince you to buy a $1,500 machine—by making it look new, putting on some shiny stuff, and showing you all the cool parts. However, you must fight to resist the "shiny" spell that they are trying to cast on you. Do not allow yourself (whether you are a parent or a student) to become entranced into making a rash commitment because of a tour. Remember, unless you stick to your guns and ask all the right questions, most college tours will show you nothing more than a lot of window dressing. Stay focused on the reasons you decided to make this visit in the first place.

A very good method for avoiding becoming blinded by the shiny luster is to make a list of things you want to see, do, and find out about. You will decide in advance on some of the items on your list based on your wants and needs. Other items will be based on statements your tour guide makes as you go along. Don't trust all the fancy descriptions, and make notes of things you want to investigate on your own. For example, a school may boast having "an extensive library and numerous computer labs around campus." Remember that these are vague descriptions, and one person's idea of "extensive" or "numerous" may not be another's. That extensive library may seem smaller in real life than it does in the school's representation—but you won't know this unless you make the effort to see it for yourself.

Visiting as many colleges as possible is going to help you learn about academic options, what type of college is the best fit for you, and what different colleges look for when awarding any kinds of scholarships, financial aid, or grant funds.

The guide may even tell you that "numerous computer labs" means four labs that serve the campus. That sounds like a lot of computers, doesn't it? Well, it could be that two of those labs only have a dozen stations. If the tour guide takes you to the main computer lab (which is the big lab that schools often show on tours), remember to ask where students can find additional labs. The tour guide may tell you, "Our campus has three more facilities that are like this one." Well, that may be true—but you won't know just how much "like this one" those other facilities are until you have physically laid eyes upon them. If this would be a selling point for you, be sure to check it out for yourself.

After the Visits

Create a college cost comparison and financial aid worksheet. Keep in mind that books, transportation, and personal expenses will not be included in your bill. In fact, the actual expenses will also vary according to your distance from the college you plan to attend and to your personal choices (and whether they are wise ones). Compare the costs of tuition, fees, housing, and meal plans for each of the colleges you visit. Add some rough estimates for variable expenses such as books, transportation, and personal expenses to each. Once that has been done, subtract the financial aid you are eligible to receive at each school. Here is an example of a college cost and financial aid comparison worksheet:

College Cost Comparison Worksheet

	College A	College B	College C	College D
Tuition				
Mandatory fees				
Housing				
Meal plans				
Total Billable Costs				
Books				
Transportation				
Personal expenses				
Total cost of attendance				
Less financial aid package				
Equals net cost to student				

Please take note that you will probably have to apply for admission at your chosen schools before you can get a financial aid package. Most colleges only determine financial aid eligibility after a student has been accepted for admission. Go ahead and do all of the financial aid paperwork for all potential institutions before their set deadlines, even if you if you have not received an official letter of acceptance or admission from them just yet.

In the Interview

Though they are not required as often as they were in past years, a face-to-face interview can serve as a second chance for students to sell themselves to the admissions office. Some students have even begun requesting personal interviews in the hopes that the extra effort will increase their chances for acceptance. Some, however, would just like an opportunity to get a first-hand look at the campus. For whatever reason, if you plan to go to an interview, you will need to be prepared.

It is best to try to schedule these interviews for either a Monday or a Friday. This way, you, and perhaps even your parents, will be able to spend the weekend before or after the interview on the campus.

FACT

If you and your family are unfamiliar with the area and do not know anyone at or near that school, it is a good idea to contact the admissions office so they can help you make arrangements for multiple-day visits. Many universities now have overnight visiting programs for prospective students.

As for the interview itself, the best thing for both you and your parents to do is to take it easy. Don't forget—you are there to find out more about the school. You are the one who has to decide if you even want to go to this school. The school is trying just as hard to make an impression on you as you are on them.

Both students and parents need to be on their best behavior when visiting a school. Dress well, have a few intelligent questions in mind (about subjects important to you), use a firm (though not vise-like) handshake, and always talk and act like you know what you're doing—even when you don't. Rehearsal interviews can also be a good prep tool, either with a parent or a teacher or guidance counselor.

With Activities, Think Quality—Not Quantity

Admissions committees are seeking more than just students with good grades. They are also eager to recruit students who are outstanding in other ways. Don't make the mistake of thinking you're an automatic "in" because you list a number of activities on your application and are therefore "well rounded." Most of the time, admissions officers are actually in search of students who as a group will make up a well-rounded population. In other words, they're looking for a diverse array of individuals with many different types of interests and abilities. By doing this, they are able to attract the interest and attention of more potential students for the future. Remember that while colleges do have minimum standards for student admissions, they have to bring in money. A smaller student body means a smaller amount of tuition being paid out by the student body as a whole—something that college administrators definitely wish to avoid.

This myth-busting truth is not necessarily a bad thing. It prevents you from having to type up a multipage list of activities to accompany your application essays, including things like the Underwater Basket-Weaving Club and the Eating Utensil Band. (Unless examples like these qualify as your primary activity, you can probably leave them out.)

However, this does not mean that you should cut down on the number of activities you participate in simply because you are concerned it will make you look bad on paper. There is a difference between applicants who are just trying to beef up their profiles by increasing the quantity of their memberships and applicants who have excelled in only a few activities—and college admissions officers have a lot of experience in telling that difference.

Though it is wise to have a broad scope of extracurricular activities, too many can cause admissions administrators to view you as unfocused, erratic, or spreading yourself too thin. This is not to say you should eliminate activities you love. Instead, you should be sure you love the activities you do.

You should not start stressing yourself out by trying to join clubs and organizations that you believe (or have heard) college admissions officers want to see listed on applications. You should do your best to avoid allowing such assumptions to control your choice of activities. It makes a lot more sense to concentrate on those activities that you are truly, passionately interested in, and strive to do your very best at them.

Knocking 'Em Dead with Your Essay

Your grade point average, name and address, and your SAT or ACT score do not give admissions officers any relevant information about the kind of human being or student you are. This is why school admissions offices often ask for essays to accompany student applications. This is your big chance to dazzle them by showing them who you are and what you have done in life. However, you must not try to make yourself sound like anyone other than who you really are (as long as you do so within the boundaries of proper grammar and correct spelling).

Common Essay Questions

Essay questions vary from one university or college to the next. It is in your best interest to have a few essays of varying subject matter ready just in case you need a generic essay to submit for admission or aid award applications. Below you will find a list of sample essay questions similar to those commonly asked on applications or in interviews by certain university admissions administrators:

- What is your idea of the perfect adventure?
- What do you value the most in relationships? Why do you think that you feel this way?
- You have just finished writing your 300-page autobiography. Please describe page 225.
- Talk about the one person you feel the closest to and tell us what you think makes your bond with this person a strong one.
- If you could declare your own holiday, what would it celebrate? Why? How would you have people observe it?

What to Write About in Admissions Essays

The truth is, if you're a student applicant, you're better off just writing about what you know than you are trying to pass yourself off as a person or personality type that you have never been. "To thine own self be true," wrote Shakespeare. How true his words are. It does you no good to write out a four-page essay on why you chose to be a music major if you honestly do not know these reasons yourself. If you find that you truly don't know the answer to a question, you might write a four-page paper about the reasons for your questions and how you feel that attending this school will help you find the answer to this inner debate.

Don't you hate it when you meet someone who only seems to be trying to impress everyone? Well, admissions officers do too. Don't try to do, say, or write what you think they want to hear. Just be you. Do what you think is right, and say what you believe.

For extra advice or coaching on how to prepare and compose a college admissions essay, think about consulting with your teachers or guidance counselors at your high school. (An English teacher would likely be most helpful, at least as a proofreader.)

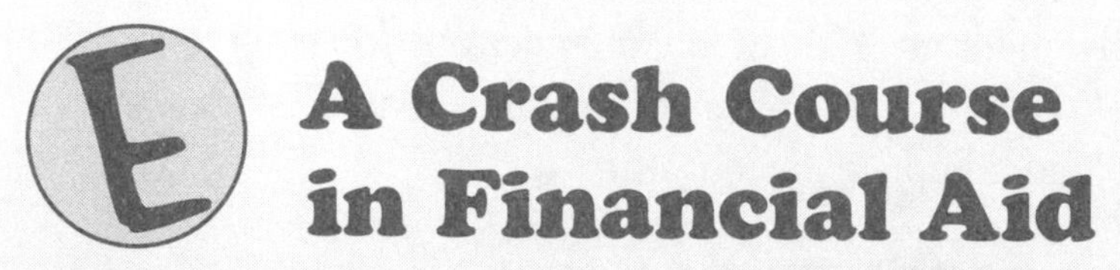

Chapter 5

A Crash Course in Financial Aid

Financial aid is always available to those who want or need it. However, the amount of aid you receive (and whether you end up getting any at all) depends on how much paperwork you are willing to sort through and how well you understand the requirements. The best way to avoid hassles is to know exactly what information you need and have it with you.

The Ins and Outs of the FAFSA Process

The acronym FAFSA stands for "Free Application for Federal Student Aid." What exactly is a FAFSA? It sounds like the name for some new cola. No, friends, the FAFSA is not quite so tasty. In fact, the FAFSA process can be downright infuriating, pushing some to the edge of a mental breakdown. If you're applying for any type of aid, chances are you'll get to know this form well—most colleges and universities require that all students applying for any kind of aid complete it each year.

How Does the FAFSA Work?

The information you put on the FAFSA is entered into a formula called the Federal Need Analysis Methodology (or just "federal methodology" for short), which measures the financial strength of your family unit. There are actually three different formulas. One is for dependent students, and two are for independent students (one for students with dependents other than a spouse, and another for students who have no dependents other than a spouse). The central processing system (CPS) uses these formulas to calculate what is called an "expected family contribution" (or EFC) for each applicant. This is the amount of money that the federal government determines your family should pay toward your education.

Applicants should never use someone else's information when filling out the FAFSA. Each individual student is required to complete his or her own application. Failure to do so could result in the denial, reduction, or revocation of benefits.

The Expected Family Contribution (EFC)

An applicant's expected family contribution, or EFC, is a determination, made with the federal methodology, of the amount of money that the family unit should be expected to contribute toward the higher education of the student. It is not necessarily what you *will* pay. Rather, this expected amount gives financial aid administrators a figure to work with when determining your aid. You may actually end up paying more or less than the calculated EFC.

This EFC formula has two parts: the parents' portion and the student's portion. Each portion is based on a formula that includes both the family members' continuous income from the prior calendar year as well as their owned assets. Parents and students simply enter their information onto the form, submit it, and the formula automatically calculates the student's EFC.

The EFC for two college students who are in the same family will most likely be slightly different because the student portion will be unique for each of them as individual applicants. It is highly unlikely that both students would end up with exactly the same income and assets.

The Parent Portion

The parent portion of the EFC is based on the parents' adjusted available income, which is a combination of available income and a portion of the parents' assets. First, the formula takes the parents' available income listed on the FAFSA (both taxed and untaxed income) and subtracts certain allowances for nondiscretionary expenses (such as taxes and minimal living expenses). The amount that is subtracted from available income is determined according to a special table in the formula that considers the number of parents and college students in the household.

Next, the parents' assets are considered. Not all assets are counted in determining the adjusted available income. A portion is protected based on the age of the older parent, according to another table in the formula. The federal methodology for the academic year 2004–2005 dictates that remaining assets be multiplied by 12 percent. Once the available income and assets contribution are calculated and added together to get the adjusted available income, a formula is used to determine the parent portion of the expected family contribution.

What investments are not counted on the FAFSA?
On the FAFSA, investments do not include your principal place of residence, the value of life insurance policies, retirement plans, prepaid tuition plans, and cash, savings, and checking account balances reported in other questions.

The Student Portion

The student's portion of the FAFSA, though oftentimes lower, is of substantial importance. The student's available income is determined by taking his or her total income (again, both taxed and untaxed), and then subtracting certain allowances. Some of the income protection allowances for figuring out the student's portion are different than those that are made for the parents.

For example, in the 2003–2004 calculation, the first $2,380 of a student applicant's income is protected. This means that anything a student earns up to that amount is not counted toward the expected family contribution. Also different is the fact that, unlike the contribution calculation for the parents' portion, there is absolutely no protection for a student applicant's assets. All of a student applicant's total assets (meaning cash, savings and checking account balances, investments, and business net worth that are not part of the student's occupational/regular income) are counted at 35 percent.

Once the parents' portion and the student's portion of the EFC are determined, they are added together to get the total EFC for the student's upcoming academic year. That amount will be the same regardless of what institution the student decides to attend. However, you should remember that your FAFSA total does not necessarily determine exactly what you end up paying toward your tuition.

Do not forget to count as untaxed income any payments you made to tax-deferred pension and savings plans, whether paid directly or withheld from your earnings. These are usually reported in box 12 of W-2 tax forms with codes D, E, F, G, H, and S. Untaxed contributions to IRA, SEP, SIMPLE, and Keogh accounts also count as untaxed income.

Learning to Understand the FAFSA Form

FAFSA, CPS, EFC, SAR—nonsense words like these may sound like a lot of fancy alphabet-soup combinations to you. However, these are some of the common acronyms found in the realm of college student financial aid. Learn what the abbreviations on the FAFSA stand for, and never assume that they mean what you think they do.

One of the most crucial elements on the FAFSA form is the amount of the student's and the parents' incomes and assets. Be as accurate as you possibly can in your estimations. You are obligated to give actual amounts, or the most accurate estimation, if actual amounts are not available. Remember, completing the FAFSA is like taking a snapshot of your financial situation on the day you complete the form.

The combined family incomes and assets are not all that matters in the calculation. The formula also considers the number of people living in the family household as well as the number of students in that household who are going to be attending college in the upcoming academic year.

Read the Instructions—Beforehand!

Be sure to read over the FAFSA instructions carefully. This will help you figure out what different terms mean in the financial aid world as well as assist you in avoiding needless mistakes. For example, in cases where the student's parents are now divorced, the term "parents" on the FAFSA form means whichever one is considered the custodial parent, as well as the student's stepparent, if any. And "investments" includes many of the things you would think, such as stock portfolios and savings accounts, but it does not include money in retirement accounts or the value of the home you live in. Be sure to pay attention to the federal financial aid definitions so you do not put down the wrong information.

Some of the key items on the FAFSA that are taken into consideration include the following: both the student's and the parents' income and assets, the number of people in the household, and the number of students in the household who will be attending college in the upcoming year.

What the FAFSA Does Not Do

The FAFSA does not take into consideration any special financial circumstances of the individual family unit. Extraordinary medical expenses or one or both parents' recent loss of a job would be examples of this. If there is anything about your family's situation that you think might be considered as a special circumstance by institution administrators, it might be a good idea for you to write a letter explaining your situation and send a copy of it to every school's financial aid office. By doing this, you allow the financial aid administrators access to information that the FAFSA does not provide to them. This gives them a chance to determine whether to consider the information you have provided as relevant to the award of financial aid. If an institution decides to use professional judgment in considering your special situation, it can then alter your expected family contribution by adjusting one or more of the input items on your FAFSA. These adjustments are made according to the estimates arrived at by evaluating your circumstances.

Filling Out the FAFSA

You can either complete the FAFSA on paper (and send it in by mail), or you can speed things up by filling it out online. The online application is often a much better option than dealing with the paper version. Both you and the schools that you list on the form will receive your results much sooner, and there is also a greatly reduced chance for making errors.

Regardless of the method you use, paper or electronic, both the student and one parent must sign the form. Obviously, if you complete the paper version, you can sign with a good old blue or black pen. If you use the online version, you have a couple of different options for signing the form. You can print the signature page, sign it in pen, and mail it in (again, mail slows the process), or you can sign electronically, using a personal identification number (PIN).

Getting a PIN and doing the online FAFSA is a good idea. Not only does it speed up your FAFSA results, but you can also use your PIN for other important things, such as accessing the National Student Loan Data System to view a history of your student loans. If you end up attending a college or university that participates in the direct loan program, then you can use your PIN to access your direct loan account information, and to e-sign your master promissory note. Getting a PIN is quick and easy. Just apply on the Web site (*www.FAFSA.ed.gov*) and wait three days. You will receive an e-mail telling you how to retrieve your PIN electronically, or you can elect to wait seven to ten days and receive the PIN in the mail.

The PIN you use to sign your FAFSA is good for life. Theoretically, a college student could get a PIN now and, in about twenty-five years, when he has a child of college age, use the same PIN to sign as the parent on his child's FAFSA.

FAFSA Deadlines—Meet Them or Miss Out

The federal deadline for filing the FAFSA isn't until June 30 of the year *after* your college attendance begins. (For example, the deadline for the 2004–2005 academic year is June 30, 2005.) However, if you want to be considered for all possible types of aid, you need to fill out the form much sooner. Remember that this one form is used by many different entities to consider you for aid. To be considered for state grants, you have to complete the FAFSA by the state's deadline, and an institution's deadline for completing the FAFSA is probably much earlier than the state's. Most colleges these days have a FAFSA filing deadline that lies somewhere between February 15 and March 15 prior to the year of academic attendance.

Because of the variety of due dates and deadlines, it is a good idea to find out the earliest FAFSA deadline at all the schools you are interested in and consider that your deadline. Filing the FAFSA by the earliest deadline will help you avoid being left out of the loop. There is such a thing as filing too early, however. Applicants are not allowed to file the FAFSA before January 1 of the academic year in which they will be attending college.

Tax Returns and the FAFSA

It is ideal for applicant families to have both the student's and the parents' tax returns for that fiscal year already completed and filed with the Internal

Revenue Service. Sometimes, however, a family can't get this done before the FAFSA deadline. In this case, schools still recommend that you complete the FAFSA form by the deadline, using the estimated information that you do have. This information can then at least be put on file, meaning it will be less of a paperwork burden later on down the road. Online applicants and their parents can easily update their information with their actual, after-taxes figures at a later time.

Updating and Correcting the FAFSA

After your FAFSA information is processed, the result you receive is called a Student Aid Report (SAR) acknowledgement. It is important for you to review the information on your SAR and make any necessary corrections or updates as soon as possible or to notify your financial aid administrator to make these changes. Accurate information is necessary in order for you to receive the financial aid you are entitled to.

Updating Financial Information

There are a couple of ways to update your information. If you filled out the FAFSA on paper, you can mark your corrections on the SAR that you received in the mail and send the form back to the federal processor. If you completed the FAFSA online, then you can go back to the Web and correct your information. You can also contact each college and university that received a report and inform them of your updated information. They can make the corrections for you.

Schools are required to use accurate FAFSA information when awarding aid. They are also required to verify a certain percentage of student FAFSAs. Don't be surprised if you get a request to submit your tax returns or other financial documents so the school can verify their accuracy.

Sending the Information to Colleges

Applicants are allowed to have their FAFSA results sent to up to six schools. To send your results to more than six schools, you should opt to use the online version—it is a much quicker and easier way to add schools. Just wait a couple of days, and then do a FAFSA correction, replacing the schools you originally listed with new ones. If you have filed the FAFSA on paper and you decide you want to have more schools receive your info, you will need to replace the schools on your SAR and mail the form back to the federal processor.

Another way to get your financial information to a college or university that you did not list originally is to provide the financial aid office with a hard copy of your SAR. (You can print one from the FAFSA Web site if you applied online.) The hard copy must include something called your data release number. When you provide a school with a copy of this information, you are also giving them your permission to request your FAFSA information for themselves.

More and more institutions are developing secure Web-based systems and procedures for delivering financial aid information to students. Soon, you may not receive paper copies of your financial aid award package from colleges and universities. Be sure you keep a working e-mail address. Check your inbox often, and notify all institutions of any changes to your e-mail address.

No matter how you add schools to your FAFSA, the schools you add will replace schools you listed originally. In other words, the original schools will stop receiving updates when they are replaced with other schools. That's not really a problem, though. If you have provided an institution with any one version of your FAFSA in a given year, they can request the updated versions. In subsequent years, you will only need to put the one school you are attending on the FAFSA, making this part of the process a lot easier.

What Is a Financial Aid Package?

A financial aid "package" is basically a list of all of the available financial aid that a particular student applicant qualifies for at a particular institution. (This determination is often based upon an applicant's FAFSA results.) Usually, the financial aid package comes in the mail, in the form of a long letter explaining the various types of financial aid options listed in the package.

The Contents of a Financial Aid Package

The items included in a financial aid package are basically a compilation of the different options that a student applicant qualifies for. A student may choose from the options offered by that particular school The options may include some of the following types of aid:

- Pell grant
- Supplemental Educational Opportunity Grant (SEOG)
- Academic or athletic scholarship
- Federal work study
- State grant
- Stafford or Direct Student loan
- Perkins loan

Of course, the student is in no way required to accept any or all of these options. These types of aid are discussed in detail throughout this book (in particular, Chapters 6, 8, 9, and 11), so don't worry if these terms mean nothing to you at this point.

FACT

You must be at least one of the following to be considered an independent student: twenty-four years old or older; enrolled in a master's or doctorate program; the parent of children who receive more than half their support from you; responsible for dependents other than your children or spouse who receive from than half their support from you; the child of parents who are both deceased (or a ward of the court/state at the age of eighteen); or a veteran of the U.S. Armed Forces.

There is no rule, regulation, or law (written or otherwise) saying that a student is forbidden to refuse to accept the loans offered to him or her in a financial aid package. Chances are, though, that if you're reading this book, you're ready to take all the help you can get. Just keep in mind that you do have the right to reject any of the items listed in a financial aid package. Whether you make use of that right is completely up to you.

How Many Packages Will We Get?

In the same way that every institution has its own financial aid office, different schools also have their own respective policies for awarding financial aid packages. This means that if you were to apply for a financial aid package at six different institutions of higher learning, you would probably receive six very different financial aid packages. Most schools require that you apply for admission, and be accepted, before they will determine your financial aid package, so remember to do that too! (Go back and read Chapter 4 if you need help with the process of applying for admission.)

Financial Aid Packages—A Diverse World

The expected family contribution (EFC) that is calculated for an applicant for the upcoming academic year is a fixed amount. This means that an applicant cannot change it, regardless of what college he or she eventually ends up attending. However, as you learned in Chapter 2, the factor that does vary is the actual cost of attendance at the various institutions you are considering. As a result of those costs, the demonstrated financial need for the student varies from one institution to another.

FACT

The total amount of a student applicant's demonstrated financial need is calculated by subtracting the expected family contribution (EFC) from the institution's total cost of attendance (COA). In other words, financial need equals COA minus EFC.

Packages Can Vary from School to School

Each college's respective financial aid office will award as much money to a student applicant as the student is qualified to receive. This qualification is based upon the individual student's demonstrated financial need *at that school.* Remember, each school has a different cost of attendance, so a student may get extremely different total financial aid amounts for different schools.

Here's an example. Suppose your EFC is calculated to be $2,000. Let's say you apply to School A, where the cost of attendance is $10,000, and to School B, where the cost of attendance is $30,000. Here is what the two financial aid packages might look like:

School A:
Pell grant: $2,100
Federal work study: $1,500
State grant: $500
Federal Stafford loan: $2,625
Federal Perkins loan: $1,000
Total aid: $7,725
Difference that family must pay or borrow for School A: $2,275

School B:
Academic scholarship: $10,000
College need-based grant: $5,000
Pell grant: $2,100
Supplemental Educational Opportunity Grant (SEOG): $1,500
Federal work study: $2,000
State grant: $3,300
Federal Stafford loan: $2,625
Federal Perkins loan: $2,000
Total aid: $28,525
Difference that family must pay or borrow at School B: $1,475

Even though School B looks more expensive at the outset, with financial aid packages like these, it will actually be more affordable for the student to attend School A.

Will Qualifications Change If You Change Schools?

As a student applicant, you can qualify for certain forms of financial aid that will remain in place regardless of what school(s) you attend between freshman year and graduation. This is true as long as your financial need does not change from one year to the next. For example, your Pell grant would not change as long as you were a full-time student at some college and as long as your EFC is the same each year you complete the FAFSA.

However, there are other monetary amounts that might end up differing as you go from one school's financial aid options to another's. This includes options such as the SEOG (Supplemental Educational Opportunity Grant), state grants, scholarship awards, work-study programs, and tuition loans. Check with each school's financial aid office to see whether your package will be affected.

Some schools may require additional forms before they award financial aid, such as the College Scholarship Service (CSS) profile. There is a nominal registration fee to complete the CSS profile and a per-school fee to send the results to institutions. So make sure a school requires the form before you pay for it and have the information sent to them. See *http://profileonline.collegeboard.com* for more information.

How Financial Administrators Award Aid

Some of the items in the financial aid package are actually awards from what are referred to as "campus-based" programs, such as the Supplemental Educational Opportunity Grants, federal work study programs, and Perkins loans. These are federal financial aid programs that are administered directly by the financial aid offices at each participating school. In other words, the institution gets an allotment from the U.S. federal government. It is up to the school to distribute the funds, and each institution can determine how it allocates the money it receives to its students (according to a set of a few short, very basic guidelines). That is why a student might end up receiving different amounts of these funds, depending upon what school the package comes from. When a school uses up its allocation for that academic year, the money is gone, and no more awards can be given out from the program that year.

Also, when it comes to financial aid funds, institutions are not very tightly regulated concerning how they spend their own money. As a result, different schools have very different amounts of money set aside in their budgets for student financial aid. Different institutions will also have their own policies for just how they think that money should be spent. In other words, a student might be awarded a large institutional scholarship in one school's financial aid package but absolutely no scholarship award whatsoever at another.

If a student qualifies for additional grants or scholarships after a financial aid package has been determined, it may affect some of the existing aid. In some cases, existing aid must be adjusted to stay within amounts allowed by federal regulations. It is a good idea to ask each institution you are considering what their policy is regarding outside scholarships.

It is always a smart idea to hold off on evaluating the bottom-line costs at different schools until after you have received the financial aid packages from all of your schools. Why? With all the facts in front of you, you can make a truly informed decision—one based upon the actual cost (the cost you pay) to attend the different schools you are considering.

Grad Students Use the FAFSA Too

The financial aid process for the adult graduate student is pretty much the same as for an undergraduate student. The main different is that a student in graduate or professional school is automatically considered to be independent, so the parents' income no longer counts toward financial aid calculations.

Graduate-level students who wish to receive federal financial aid or grants must file a FAFSA stating that they are pursuing a master's or doctorate degree (or have entered some other graduate study program). To continue receiving aid, students must indicate the same continuing education on the FAFSA renewal forms. Graduate level students are also eligible to receive Stafford loans, Perkins loans, and Federal work study. This means filling out a FAFSA is definitely in your best interests. After all, every little bit helps!

Chapter 6

Scholarships: Something for Everyone

Scholarships are a good way to ease the financial burden of paying for college. They're not as big a paperwork fiasco as federal loans can be, and plenty of them are available. However, scholarship applicants must be ambitious, since it is up to them to seek out and apply for awards. Each scholarship requires applicants to meet certain criteria. However, even if they meet all the criteria, applicants should not expect to simply be handed a scholarship. A good deal of work is involved, as you will soon see.

Scholarship Basics

Once you start looking for scholarships to qualify for, you will discover that there are as many types of scholarships as there are types of students. Frequently, a scholarship comes with eligibility requirements that tailor it to students of a particular background. Many scholarships are geared toward an applicant's major, while others reward athletic ability. For some, the applicant's parents determine the student's eligibility (such as scholarships for children of veterans). Still other scholarships are awarded on the basis of a student's social, ethnic, or religious background, such as scholarships from the United Negro College Fund, or on the student's gender or sexual orientation, like those made available only to women or only to transgender students.

What Is a Scholarship?

Scholarships are usually awards that do not have to be paid back, given for the purpose of aiding in payment of education costs. Sometimes, scholarship foundations or the individual donors for a scholarship will attach certain requirements that a student must meet to receive and keep the scholarship. If the student fails to fulfill these requirements after the scholarship has been awarded, the money must be paid back. In some cases, failing to meet requirements may result in the scholarship being reverted into the form of a loan—as Pennsylvania does with its NETS (New Economy Technology Scholarships) program.

Will It Pay for Everything?

Some scholarships are guaranteed to remain in effect for a certain length of time or for a specified number of semesters. Some might even last for the entire duration of a student's enrollment, all the way up to the completion of the bachelor's degree. Some scholarships expire after a certain length of time, but these may also be renewable. If the student applies again at the end of the award term and can provide evidence that all the minimum criteria requirements continue to be met or even exceeded (such as a specified level of athletic performance or a minimum GPA), that student may continue to receive the scholarship for an additional term.

Scholarship applications often require additional documents, such as a high school transcript, letter of recommendation, an essay, or a copy of the student's federal Student Aid Report (SAR) before the application is considered complete. Review the application requirements carefully, and be sure to include all required supporting documents.

Other scholarships are exclusively one-time awards. Don't view that as a bad thing—money that pays for your education is always a good thing; don't turn up your nose at it because it comes in the form of a single lump sum. Scholarships range in value from hundreds of dollars to thousands, and in some cases have been known to pay for an individual's entire tuition bill.

Scholarships Versus Grants

Try hard not to confuse a scholarship with a grant. Unfortunately, this is a lot easier said than done. The terms "scholarship" and "grant" are sometimes used interchangeably, even by those parties who award them, and this has become the cause for a lot of confusion about the actual differences between the two. More often than not, scholarships are awarded based upon some form of outstanding achievement or something else that makes the student stand apart from others (such as athletic ability, artistic or musical talent, or life experience), whereas most grants are based solely upon a student's financial need.

The Most Common Types of Scholarships

While there are scores of different scholarship types to be found out there, some are more common than others. Roughly speaking, scholarships come in two main categories: those based on merit and those based on need. Merit-based scholarships can be broken down even further into subgroups such as gender-based, academic, and athletic.

FACT

Institutional scholarships are those that are made available by the college to which students are applying. They can be awarded upon admission or applied for after acceptance and throughout a student's enrollment. Noninstitutional scholarships are all other awards that come from outside the college or university.

Gender-Based Scholarships—Male or Female?

Some scholarships are based on an applicant's gender. Don't rule these out as an option—find out what the school you are interested in offers. Athletic scholarship regulations permit Division I and II colleges to offer more male or more female scholarships in different sports, so the chances of being awarded an athletic scholarship for a particular sport might be better for male players, while another sport may offer more scholarships for females. Female students should not overlook schools with more scholarships for males. The scholarships that are awarded to female student-athletes may be substantially larger than those from a school where such scholarships are commonplace.

While some of the more obscure scholarships might not be what you would normally think of as big-dollar financial aid, obtaining even a few of them could add up to significant money. Three $500 scholarships add up to $1,500 and, to most people, that is quite a bit of money. Remember that every dollar you can get in scholarship money is money you don't have to borrow—meaning less money you will have to eventually pay back.

Athletics Versus Academics—The Battle for Money

Almost all institutions of higher learning have academic scholarship programs. Depending on the scholarship, eligibility is based on a student's high school academic achievement and test scores or on academic excellence as a college student. Schools often have much more flexibility in the way they administer these academic scholarship programs than they do for athletic scholarships. This is because the National Collegiate Athletics Association (NCAA), along with the other athletic conferences, has a laundry list of rules and regulations regarding the award of athletic scholarships. These rules are often based upon what athletic division the school belongs to and in what sport(s) they host teams.

Some sports that fall into NCAA Divisions I and II are restricted in the number of scholarships the institution is allowed to award, whereas NCAA Division III schools are completely forbidden from recognizing athletic ability with scholarships. So, apparently the old myth about how athletics are favored over academics when it comes to scholarships is unfounded—at least at some schools.

Merit-Based Versus Need-Based

While some scholarships are based on academic, artistic, humanitarian, or athletic merits, others are based solely upon a student's financial need. There are some scholarships, however, that recognize both merit and financial need, so do not rule out anything that you might qualify for.

An example of a scholarship program that recognizes both academics and financial need is the Kansas State Scholarship. Between 1,000 and 1,500 scholarships are given out annually to students who are Kansas residents with a minimum 3.0 GPA who have demonstrated financial need. Applications, FAFSAs, test scores, and transcripts are required of all applicants.

Always know what the terms and/or limitations of a scholarship are before you apply. Remember, meeting the criteria at application does not guarantee you will be able to meet the ongoing requirements to keep the scholarship.

Financial need, especially, can be seen from a number of very different perspectives that change from one scholarship donor or committee to the next. One scholarship committee might base its evaluation of an applicant on demonstrated financial need as determined by the federal government. However, another donor might consider an applicant "needy" simply because there is not already enough scholarship and/or grant money to cover the cost of a higher education.

Many institutions and private sources have scholarships for students with outstanding high school academic records. If there is no mention of the student's or parents' income or asset information on the application materials, you can assume that financial need is not among the criteria.

Welcome to the Scholarship Jungle!

Yes, it is a cliché, but it's true—it is a jungle out there! Looking for the right scholarship can make anyone start to feel a little bit overwhelmed. How are you supposed to decide which scholarships to apply for? How do you know if you have a better chance of getting one than another?

Well, the first thing anyone who plans to find a scholarship needs to do is to make out a list of "possibles." This means making a list of all scholarships that you are qualified to receive. You might not necessarily be applying for all of them, so feel free make this list as long as you can.

Some scholarships are based on merit, others on need, and some recognize both. Do not rule out anything that you even remotely qualify for. Financial need, especially, is defined by different standards by different scholarship donors. Some might base their evaluation upon demonstrated financial need as determined by the government through the FAFSA (Free Application for Federal Student Aid). Other scholarship committees might consider you "needy" just because you do not already have enough scholarships and/or grant money to cover the cost of your education.

When searching for scholarship opportunities, do not apply for scholarships that require you to choose a major you are not interested in. It's a bad idea to choose educational goals and a career path that are not a good fit for you, no matter how much money the scholarship is worth.

Rather than ruling something out because you aren't positive you qualify, take a chance and fill it out. It only takes a little time (relatively speaking) to fill out a scholarship application. Think about it this way. Let's say it takes you four hours to complete an application for something as small as a $100 scholarship. If you get it, that's the equivalent of $25 an hour for your work—pretty good money for a high school student who gets $6 an hour to clean out grease vats at the local fast-food joint.

How Do I Find Available Scholarships?

Students and parents should think of themselves as private investigators when searching for scholarship opportunities. Don't leave any stone unturned when it comes to finding awards that you might qualify for. Ask at each school you are interested in. Do a little Internet surfing. Sign up for a free membership with a few scholarship-savvy Web sites that have good search engines for scholarships, such as *www.fastweb.com*, *www.petersons.com*, or *www.collegeboard.com*. Keep a sharp eye on the local newspaper. Check with various state and federal agencies. If nothing else—ask around!

Visit the Guidance Counselor's Office

It is a guidance counselor's job to help students with matters concerning what they plan to do after graduation. Therefore, scholarships should be among any guidance counselor's specialties. Make it a point to apply for any scholarships that you can find through your guidance counselor, as these are often focused specifically toward high school students.

Few guidance counselors have the time to hunt down individual students to tell them when a new scholarship opportunity becomes available. However, if they have seen your face often enough to be able to put your name with it, they just might hunt you down. It is up to you as a student to stay on top of what scholarships are available throughout your senior year.

You live in a world that now has the Internet. So, for goodness sakes, use it! Among the information available is a seemingly endless number of scholarships. Some scholarships even have online applications. You can apply for these with nothing more than a short e-mail essay.

Look Where You Live

Check in the local community as well. Some local health-care agencies, for instance, offer scholarships to college students who plan to study nursing. In return, the student agrees to a work obligation for a certain period of time, either during or after the educational program.

There are also service organizations, such as parent-teacher organizations, athletic associations, the Elks Club, Kiwanis, Lions Club, and so on, that may offer scholarships for deserving students in the surrounding community. Keep an eye on the local newspaper for possible scholarship information.

Some scholarship foundations designate banks to manage scholarship funds. You or your parents might want to contact some of the local nonprofit organizations or even their bank representatives to inquire about possible scholarships.

You Will Qualify for At Least One

If someone says that they were unable to get a scholarship because they did not qualify for any, they are not being truthful to you (or to themselves, most likely). The same goes for applications. "There aren't any scholarships that I qualify to even apply for," is about as true as saying, "I don't have anything to wear." Neither of these statements is true. There is always something to wear; you just do not want to wear what you have. In the same way, there are always scholarships you qualify for; you just need to be willing to do the work.

Don't Rule Out School Programs

All colleges are different, and their scholarship programs are just as different from one school to the next. One institution might offer only a handful of scholarships to its best-qualified applicants, while another institution may have the funds to offer several hundred separate scholarships. A student might get a full-tuition scholarship at one college and not be awarded as much as a dime at another. If you haven't made a final decision yet on which college or university to attend, don't rule out the idea of checking with the financial aid departments of several schools. See what kind of scholarships they offer and whether they fit you. Just because you're not eligible for any scholarships at one school doesn't mean you won't find the perfect fit at the next.

Don't Give Up

It is not enough to do one simple Internet search before you decide to give up. If you have trouble finding enough possible scholarships after one search, modify your search terms and try again.

Beware of scholarship scams! Scholarships should not cost you any money whatsoever. Nor should you be expected at any time to provide information such as your credit card number or bank account number in order for a donor to put a "hold" on your scholarship so that it is not awarded to someone else.

Scholarship opportunities are available to students from a variety of sources—the federal government, colleges to which a student is applying, private scholarship donors, businesses, nonprofit organizations, and philanthropic foundations. Some of the Greek social organizations (fraternities and sororities) and honor societies offer scholarships. Investigate possible opportunities in these areas if you are a member. Check out both local and national scholarship possibilities. Be sure you understand that at this point, these are nothing more than opportunities. Scholarships do not just come to you, and application is not a guarantee of an award.

Scholarships Parents Can Apply For

Sometimes, when trying to get a scholarship, *what* you know is not nearly as important as *who* you know. Other times, it's even more important to figure out who your parents know—more specifically, where your parents work and what they have done in their lives. Does this mean that parents should try to use their personal influences to squeeze out scholarship money for their kids? Not necessarily—in fact, many parents simply don't need to.

Employee Scholarships

If you are a parent, your place of employment may offer scholarships or grants to your children simply because you are an employee. If you are a prospective student, you might want to ask your parents about checking to see whether their employers sponsor such programs.

For example, United Technologies Corporation (or UTC, owner of aerodynamics manufacturing giant Pratt & Whitney) has established a scholarship program meant to assist the children of employees planning to pursue higher education at a college or university. These renewable scholarships are offered in the amount of $3,000 each year and are awarded for the term of that year for full-time study at an accredited four-year college or university of the student's choice.

These awards are given for undergraduate study only, and renewal is limited to no more than three additional years (for a total of four years) or until the student has completed a bachelor's degree—whichever happens first. Renewal is decided based upon whether the student displays satisfactory academic performance in a full-time course of study and whether UTC continues the program.

FACT

Although many employers now offer college scholarships or even full tuition grants for the children or dependents of employees, be sure you check the fine print. Most of the time, the employee must be active and working full-time, and the student dependent must attend a four-year study program at an accredited university to receive the award.

Even if you are not an employee of the abovementioned company, your employer may have a similar program. For instance, GTE hosts a similar program. There are even scholarships available to the children of public school employees. Remember that it never hurts to ask about scholarships, and you cannot know if they exist without asking. Parents should contact their employers' human resources departments to find out if they host such a program. If so, schedule an appointment with a representative or request materials that include any further details.

Children of Veterans Scholarships

More scholarships are available to the children of veterans than you can shake a stick at. Some universities, such as the University of Illinois, actually host Children of Veterans scholarship programs—with scholarship money specifically set aside for the children of military veterans.

There is also a Children of Vietnam Veterans Scholarship fund, with a collective total of $100,000 in scholarships awarded each year. The American Legion Auxiliary National President's Scholarship is also awarded solely to the children of veterans who served in the U.S. Armed Forces, as are the Amvets' Scholarships.

If you are a dependent (that is, a child or a spouse) of an active duty member of any branch of the U.S. Armed Forces, the federal government will pay for as much as 75 percent of your tuition costs.

Consider Applications and Requirements Individually

No two scholarship applications are identical. The work that you have to put in to complete those applications is as diverse as the scholarships being offered. At the scholarship-savvy FastWeb site, for example (*www.fastweb.com*), students can register their unique student profile free of charge and find information on hundreds of scholarships, internships, and grants. The profile asks questions that, once submitted, are compared with the criteria for thousands of scholarships. Those that come back as matches are then compiled and listed on the student's account. However, because many scholarships have multiple eligibility requirements, you will not qualify for all the matches that your search returns. It will take a lot of time and perseverance, whether you work online or by more old-fashioned methods (such as the library), to find scholarships that are completely suited to your needs.

They All Take Time

Students and parents should expect to spend a certain amount of time and effort searching out and applying for scholarships. As a student, you must also understand that there is a good possibility that you will have to write a different essay every time you apply for a new scholarship.

Be sure to make of copies of all your scholarship applications, as well as your scholarship essays, and keep them in a folder. Sometimes you can modify these essays and applications and make them work for more than just one scholarship application. Chapter 7 explains in detail how to put together a winning scholarship application.

Is online scholarship application easier?
Simply put—no, not really. All kinds of scholarships are available online for students of all backgrounds, abilities, interests, and needs. However, when you find a scholarship that you are eligible to apply for, you should still be prepared to compile the necessary information.

Are You Eligible?

As you begin to search through scholarship application forms, you may find some with long or detailed lists of eligibility requirements. Do not let the detailed criteria of a scholarship discourage you; instead, fill out an application for anything that remotely seems to fit you or your student. Even if a scholarship application lists both merit- and need-based criteria, the selection committee might weigh one factor much more heavily than the other. A scholarship applicant who is not exactly stellar academically (meaning a GPA of less than the almighty 4.0) with verifiable financial need might be awarded a scholarship over a much more academically qualified applicant with less financial need, or vice versa. Applying for scholarships doesn't cost you anything, so if you think it's possible you might be considered, send in an application. You have nothing to lose and only money to gain.

Chapter 7

Have a Killer Scholarship Application!

Scholarship applications can sometimes be hard to wrap your head around. After all, who knows what exactly constitutes a "good" application? Is an essay's subject content more valuable than its grammatical correctness? Just how important are good grammar and spelling? Where do you find the line between making yourself sound good and lying outright? All of these are very valid questions, each of which will be covered in the following pages.

What Applicants Should Do

Before getting into the big "no-no's" of filling out a scholarship application, it's a good idea to figure out the basic stuff that applicants *should* do. After all, failing to complete a requirement can be just as damaging as doing something that you should not do. Here is an acronym to help you remember what to do—PILS. (Think of it as a prescription.) PILS stands for "Proofreading, Instructions, Legibility, and Significance." Which is most important? All of them. These four points are essential for keeping an application out of the wastebasket and getting it past the first cut.

Consider including a cover letter with your scholarship application, even if it is not required. A good letter may set your application apart from others by giving it a more organized and sophisticated appearance. It also gives you an opportunity to express your appreciation for being considered for the scholarship and to say a few more things about yourself.

Proofread, Then Let Someone Else Proofread

Always proofread your application! In fact, proofread it twice. Careless misspelling and improper grammar can be serious faux pas on a scholarship application. If you are not sure about a word's spelling, find yourself a dictionary and look it up. Once you have finished proofreading, it's smart to find someone, it doesn't matter who (as long as he or she is a somewhat proficient reader), to proofread your application again. Why? Well, when you read your own work, you cannot help but be a little biased about how good it is. You are also so used to looking at it by this point that you might be looking right at a mistake and not see it. Someone else might see a typo that you overlooked.

Instructions—Follow Them!

Want to put an application on the fast track to the bottom of a trash bin? All you have to do is ignore the application's written directions, and it is almost guaranteed that your packet will end up in the administrator's office shredder in no time flat! The application instructions were put there for a very good reason, and that reason may be more complicated than you think.

Avoid using big "ten-dollar" words—especially if you are not 100-percent positive you know what the big word means. For example, a phrase such as "the transparent symbology of the situation was absolutely ecstatic," would be a really bad idea (not to mention it would make zero sense). A scholarship committee will see right through this. Use real language that you understand.

A scholarship application's instructions have a dual purpose. Not only are they meant to make the lives of administrators and donors easier, but they are also designed to help evaluate what kind of student you might be. The instructions are there just as much to screen applicants as they are to help them fill the darn thing out. Failure to follow the directions on an application will demonstrate to the administrators or scholarship donors that the applicant is hasty, sloppy, and cannot even follow simple instructions. Obviously, this is not the kind of impression you want to make, so be sure to follow the directions to the letter.

Legibility—It Just Makes Sense!

Write legibly, for goodness sakes. Your best bet would be to type out your application. While sloppiness is a surefire way to make an application stand out from the pack, it is not exactly the kind of attention that an applicant wants. Although typing is preferred, hand printing is also acceptable as long as it is done neatly and legibly. Be sure to use either blue or black ink, however, if you must use a pen. (Pencil and colored ink look very unprofessional and can be difficult to read.)

If you have any interviews for scholarships, be prepared to talk about yourself. Some students are simply not prepared to have a comfortable conversation about themselves with the interviewer. It is all about you, so be comfortable with who you are, ready to talk, and have a few questions to ask the interviewer, too!

Significant Information Only, Please

With all this talk about legibility and proofreading, you may be wondering whether an application essay's subject content is valued over grammatical correctness. Here's your answer: not exactly. Both factors will probably be given as much attention as possible. However, keep in mind that sometimes, *what* you say can be either improved or destroyed by *how* you choose to say it. This is especially true when it comes to talking about yourself.

Try to include as much significant information about yourself as possible on your scholarship application. It is easy to get carried away in the passion of writing inspiration and go off on tangents that are not relevant to the situation at hand. This kind of sloppy thinking is not going to improve your application and certainly won't dazzle the administrator who has to sit there and read through it.

Information such as your position on the County Gambling Poker League should take a back seat to the kinds of things that might hold a special place in the human heart, such as volunteering for Habitat for Humanity, participating in an annual charity race or event, or even a martial arts tournament championship title. (If you have a black belt in any martial art, that would be a very good thing to list on your application—it demonstrates that you possess both determination and self-discipline.) Whatever information you decide to put on your application, just make sure that it is significant—not only to you but also to the person who will read it as well.

What Applicants Should Not Do

In Spanish, *mal* means "bad." In the list of scholarship application don'ts, it still means bad—and a whole lot more. That's right, it's time for another acronym—MAL. The letters MAL stand for the three "big, bad things" that any and all scholarship applicants should avoid doing, at all costs—"Misrepresentation, Assuming, and Lying." These three little sins can be seriously tough temptations sometimes, but they will do more harm than good—so be strong.

Miss Representation—She's Not a Beauty Queen

Do not misrepresent yourself on scholarship or college admissions essays. When applicants do this, it can often be very obvious to the reader of their applications. (Yes, that includes the person who decides whether to award you any financial aid.) Before you start listing every activity you can think of, ask yourself honestly whether you are genuinely involved and even interested in the things that you plan to write about. You might find that you're just trying to make an impression or fill up space on the application. For example, if you write that you are a volunteer for Habitat for Humanity, then you should have been involved regularly. If you gave up one Saturday morning way back in your freshman year, you probably shouldn't list this as one of your volunteer/community service activities.

Many universities and scholarship committees encourage you to include a video or other multimedia materials with your application. Remember, admissions and scholarship administrators sometimes go through thousands of applications each year. A video resume could help them to remember a student they might have otherwise inadvertently overlooked.

Don't Assume You Know What They Want

You should be an active participant in different kinds of activities because you enjoy them or (more importantly) because they give you a sense of fulfillment or personal satisfaction—not because you think it will make you look good on your college admission or scholarship applications. There are no secret clubs or activities that all (or even most) college administrators or scholarship donors look for on applications. Don't assume that there is any one thing that you must be involved with in order to receive a scholarship.

Remember that activities are not restricted to the high school campus. Applicants should be sure to include anything they participate in outside of school. A part-time job, church or charity activities, or any other form of community involvement should be included on your list of activities and interests.

Lying—Save It for April Fool's Day!

The one thing you absolutely want to avoid doing is making up information. For example, do not write on your application that you spent the last two years as the captain of the local chess team when, in all actuality, there is no local chess team. You may figure that since there was no team, it would be impossible for the administrators or donors to be sure you are telling the truth. True, your lie may slip by. But what will you do when, two years later, it is discovered that you lied on your application? When they expel you from school, yank your scholarship, and demand to be paid back what you have been awarded already, what are you going to do? Maybe you should rethink inventing that chess team before it's too late.

Making Yourself Sound Good—Without Lying!

If you want to be able to present yourself in the best possible light, try to get involved in activities that you are passionate about and list them on your application. Then make a conscious effort to use positive language when describing yourself as a person, student or otherwise. You may have heard the saying, "It's not what you say, but how you say it." You might compare this to reading a horror novel to a newborn at bedtime. It is not scary to the baby as long as you read it in a soft, comforting tone of voice. Wording your application correctly works about the same way.

Word It Right

Manipulation of words is *not* lying. Do not lie! Just word it right. For example, let's say that an essay question asks you to describe yourself. Suppose you were to write, "I find that I overestimate myself and bite off more than I can chew most of the time. However, I also find that I can get most of these things done . . . when I am finally forced to." This may be the truth, but it's not going to impress anyone. On the other hand, you could say the same thing with wording such as this: "I am a creative, energetic, and ambitious student who enjoys dashing full force into everything that I do." This sounds a whole lot better than the first example, but it still describes you.

Do Something Useful

Everyone does *something* when they're not in school or doing homework. Ask yourself, "How do I spend most of my time?" It is crucial that you have more than just a high GPA (though the GPA helps). Get involved in something. Again, this should be something that you sincerely enjoy doing, preferably something that you are somewhat passionate about. Spending your time with a one or two (or even three) genuine interests is much more valuable than joining a bunch of clubs so you can write them on your application but without ever actually showing up at a meeting.

As you will find repeated throughout the pages of this book, what you say can be greatly improved or terribly tarnished by the way in which you choose to say it. Remember that an application is not a face-to-face meeting or even a handshake. This application is a piece of paper, and its purpose is to make you a living, breathing, altogether real person in the eyes of administrators who will probably never see your face. This will be most effective if you put a good dose of passion and enthusiasm into your activity descriptions.

FACT

To maximize your institutional scholarship possibilities, apply to a variety of colleges and universities. If you apply only to institutions that are a stretch for you academically, you may not receive any scholarships at all. A range of institutions will send you a variety of financial aid packages that may give you more options.

For the sake of argument, let's say you are an avid player of role playing games (such as Magic, Vampire the Masquerade, or good ol' Dungeons and Dragons) or multiplayer video games, and that this has been your main interest, hobby, and pastime for the majority of your adolescent life. Well, you're not going to impress anybody if you describe this activity along these lines: "I spend most of my spare time either playing games with some of my friends at my mom's dining room table, or sitting in my room playing video games." Instead, tell those administrators about your hobby and throw in a good-sized chunk of gusto! Say something like, "I have spent nearly a decade improving my personal skills in the art and practice of strategy and have been instrumental in the scheduling, organization, and hosting of strategic gaming events for player groups in my local area. When not scheduling events, I am sharpening my skills with strategy exercises I can do on my own." Doesn't that sound more impressive than the first version? By writing this way, you have illustrated yourself better, painting a picture in the mind of the administrator of a sharp-witted student who displays leadership ability, organizational skills, responsibility, and self-discipline. The best thing is that you did it without lying!

What Are Administrators Looking For?

It's time for some hard reality—there are no particular activities that administrators are looking for! Instead, administrators are on the lookout for something that makes you unique and makes you stand out from the crowd. This is why it can pay off more to follow your true interests when choosing your activities.

The truth is that people tend to be a lot more transparent than they realize. If you are involved wholeheartedly in activities that matter to you, when you write about them or talk about them in an interview, you will be able to write or speak with both enthusiasm and knowledge.

Who's Writing Your Recommendation?

If you have a scholarship application that requires a letter of recommendation, ask someone who knows you well and is likely to write favorable things about you. Give the person an ample amount of time to write the recommendation letter and provide a stamped, addressed envelope if the letters are to be mailed directly to the scholarship donor to ensure authenticity. Be sure to follow up with your recommenders with a little thank-you note.

They took time out of their lives to help you, and it's always polite to show your appreciation.

Don't Leave "Activities" Blank

Okay, so you're a high school senior, just starting to look into applying for financial aid, and you haven't been involved in any sports or clubs. What can you discuss on your application? Are you still in the running for scholarship money? Students who haven't been active members in their school community or who do not belong to clubs or volunteer outside of school have done *something* in their spare time. Whatever that something is, try to make it sound as important and interesting as possible. Obviously, if you have spent a lot of time doing something (no matter what it is), it must be important to you.

Some institutions offer legacy scholarships for students with relatives who are either alumni or currently enrolled students. Ask about this possibility if you have any siblings, parents, aunts, uncles, cousins, or grandparents who have attended the same institution.

Many interests do not fit into the category of school or community activity. Reading, listening to music, jogging, or bicycling, for instance, should be listed as a hobby if that is what you enjoy. Remember to go into a little detail. For the above-mentioned activities, you might list "Reading about the Civil War," "Listening to classical music," "Running fifteen miles per week," or "Bicycling in state/national parks."

If you have a part-time job or a hobby related to your planned major, then you should emphasize your interest in that field on your application. By showing that you already have taken steps toward learning more about that subject through your activities, scholarship administrators are more likely to see that their money will help a motivated student pursue a known interest.

Be careful, however. While it is good to show that you have one or two distinct interests, you do not want to appear too narrowly focused. You can also write about your one or two interests that you have not had an opportunity to pursue yet and how scholarship money would open those doors for you. Most of all, try to appear sincere and appreciative.

How Important Is the Essay?

Again, all scholarships are not the same. Not all scholarship committees even require applicants to write an essay. Those that do are often looking for very different things, so the biggest challenge is to be so adaptable that you can make yourself look good no matter what questions they throw at you. For example, if the application appears to emphasize financial need, make an effort to go into more detail about your qualifications in that area. Explain how the scholarship will help you meet your educational goals.

If the essay question indicates that the scholarship donor wants to know how well rounded you are, then try to dig a little deeper as you start listing your activities. This will show that you have a broad range of abilities and interests (but not necessarily many in number). The most important part is to figure out what kind of student each application seems to focus on. Then fill out the application as honestly and sincerely as you can with that focus in mind.

FACT

In order to protect students and prevent scholarship fraud, the Federal Trade Commission initiated Project Scholarscam in 1996. Since then, the FTC's legal actions have resulted in a number of court orders prohibiting future fraudulent misrepresentations against eleven companies and thirty individuals.

The Price of Plagiarism

Do not plagiarize. Simply put, this is another way to send your application straight into the trash. Or worse, maybe it won't; instead, maybe your plagiarism will come back to haunt you halfway through your college career. This is a pretty simple concept—stealing work from someone else and claiming it as your own is not a good idea. It's also unethical, and the harm it can cause is far worse than the temporary benefits it may bring. Of course, ignorance of the law does not excuse breaking it, and plagiarism is no different. So be sure that you understand where the line falls between "citation of sources" and the theft of someone else's work. You would think this would be a pretty solid line—and it is—but a reminder every now and then of exactly where it falls never hurts.

Plagiarism or Common Knowledge?

The term "common knowledge" refers to facts that can be found in so many available sources that they are more than likely to be known by most people. For example, it is common knowledge that the initials "B.C." stand for "before Christ." It's common knowledge that the American Revolution was fought against the British. These are facts commonly known by just about anyone who made it through elementary school. You are not required to document common knowledge when you state it as fact.

However, you are still required to cite sources and document facts that are not commonly known. This also holds true for ideas that compile and interpret facts (though those facts themselves might be common knowledge) into a single concept, theory, or idea that is not your own. For example, if you were to write, "What goes up must come down," you would not be required to cite Isaac Newton or Albert Einstein as your sources. Why not? Because this fact is easily observable for anyone interested in noticing the world around them—much less that elementary-school education. You are not introducing anyone else's ideas or language in a way that makes it seem as if you are claiming them as your own.

However, if you were to write, "What goes up must come down, unless, through the implementation of magnetic forces, gravity is countered to the point that it is matched or defied. This has been proven." Well, this is Sir Isaac Newton's language, his theory and experiment, and therefore not yours to claim. In this case, even though you are stating a commonly known fact, you are using someone else's thoughts and language as your own. If it is not your theory, not your experiment, and therefore not yours to claim in writing, then you are plagiarizing. Consequently, you must provide supporting evidence by citing the name of the person who conducted the study, along with the where and how (and the why, if applicable).

Document your sources in standard documentation style. The MLA (Modern Language Association) Style is the most commonly accepted form of citation. You may even want to purchase the MLA Handbook.

Plagiarism and the Internet

The Internet is now probably the most popular source of information for everyone, including students. With so many sources available, a number of questions have come up regarding ways to prevent plagiarism. Copying information word for word is plagiarism, whether the source is a book, a magazine, or a Web site. The same ethical guidelines apply to the Internet and printed sources. When you refer to someone else's ideas, or you take a quotation from a printed page or a Web site, you are required to name the source. Anything else is plagiarizing. For example, if you were to go online and copy (or buy) an essay, change the wording a little bit, and then paste your name onto it, that would be blatant plagiarism.

If a writer wishes to make use of pictures, movies, images (such as graphics or photos), or musical compositions, a majority of the same rules continue to apply. If you copy visuals or graphics from an online source, this can be very much the same as quoting from a book or essay, and your source for the picture, graphic, or data has to be cited. The same rules continue to apply to other uses of visual or written data taken from Web sites. For example, if you were constructing a Web page for a computer science class and you copied pictures, graphics, or some other kind of visual information from other sites, you would be required to provide your source for each. In the case of online sources, it is best to obtain written permission from the site owner, at least in the form of an e-mail, prior to making use of those materials.

Strategies for Avoiding Plagiarism

Use quotation marks to indicate you have taken directly from the text of a book, Web site, or any other source. This is a clear way for you to show you're using someone else's thoughts in the exact words they used. You do not need to worry about quoting your own thought processes (obviously) or things that are common knowledge. This can be especially important when you are taking notes. Do not write copy anything out without also noting where it came from and who said or wrote it.

Paraphrasing is a little bit different. When you are paraphrasing, you are making use of someone else's ideas, though you are explaining them in your own words. This is a legitimate tactic that many college students use when incorporating sources into their writing. However, even though it is your words that end up on the paper, you must still cite the sources for the data you have used.

Be careful not to cross the line between paraphrasing and just rearranging or replacing a few words to try to modify someone else's words to look like your own. You may as well be playing Russian roulette. Make sure you read over everything you plan to paraphrase. Put away the book or close the Web site you are quoting as you write. This way, because you are unable to see the original language, it is a lot less likely you will plagiarize—even accidentally—by copying the source word for word.

Write out your own ideas, in your own words, without stealing from someone else's hard work. Double-check your paraphrasing against the source that you used in order to make absolutely certain that you did not "accidentally" (it can happen) use the same wording as the author.

Say "Thank You"

Here is a important note regarding scholarships: Be sure to always say thank you for any money that you receive, especially if it's possible that the award might be renewed the following year. Remember, no one *has* to give you any free money. If you are blessed enough to be awarded some, be sure to thank the person who had a hand in giving it to you. Scholarship administrators are much more likely to reconsider renewing money to a grateful, appreciative recipient than to someone who does not even have the common courtesy to send out a simple thank-you note.

Chapter 8

Getting to Know Grants

Everybody appreciates getting money, especially when it is the kind of money that helps pay your tuition bill. If you can't seem to find a scholarship that's quite right for you or you need some extra help, then a grant may be the way to go. Some grants require applicants to maintain a certain cumulative grade point average or to major in a certain field. Other grants are given only to students who can demonstrate financial need, and still others are awarded based on a work obligation or some other stipulation.

What Is a Grant?

Different people think of different things when they think of grants, which is understandable because of the lack of a precise definition and the fact that grants can be for any amount of money. Grants can be awarded to you from the federal government, your state government, the college or university that you attend, or from a number of alternative private sources. This chapter includes examples of each.

Mixing and Matching Terms

Remember that some people use the terms "scholarships" and "grants" interchangeably, as though they were the same thing. It is a good idea to keep this in mind so that you do not overlook an opportunity simply because of what the source of aid is called. For example, maybe you can't demonstrate much financial need because the expected family contribution results on your FAFSA are too high, and you don't think you're eligible to receive any grants. Suppose, then, that an engineering company offers a grant that helps toward tuition costs for any student who majors in engineering. The application for such a grant might require the student to list engineering courses that he or she has taken to the present date along with an explanation of future plans and goals. The company might not even mention (or even consider) financial need in application screenings. (This sounds a lot like a scholarship, doesn't it?) If you had overlooked this because it was called a grant, you could have missed out on extra funding for your college career.

Are Grants Better?

It doesn't matter whether the money you apply for is called a "scholarship," a "grant," or an "award." All of these terms are considered "grant assistance" in the financial aid field. Let's face it. If someone wants to give you money to help pay for your education, do you really care what they call it? The truth is that scholarships and grants are equal—neither is really better than the other. Obviously, grants *are* better than taking out loans or getting an extra job. Find out which ones you qualify for, and apply for them!

When will I find out if I qualify for any grants?
Each institution has its own particular timeline for notifying recipients of grant awards. The sooner you have completed and filed the FAFSA application, the sooner you are likely to see the results from colleges and universities. Some institutions will even do the estimates for your financial aid package early if you are willing to complete a special form or if you are considered a serious prospective student of that institution.

Pointers When Considering Grants

Some students wouldn't even bother applying for any grants simply because they believe that they don't qualify for any kind of need-based aid, and they assume that all grants are awarded based solely upon financial need. Do not be one of these people! Always apply for any financial aid for which you are even remotely qualified. The organization awarding the grant might put a higher priority on helping out a strong candidate in a certain field than they do on helping out the applicant with the greatest amount of financial need.

Applying for Grants

Like scholarships, grants can come from a variety of sources, so make sure you investigate your grant options and meet the application requirements. For example, to apply for federal grants, you just need to complete the FAFSA by the school's deadline. To apply for state grants, you must complete all the required forms by the state deadline. Know what these deadlines are for your institution and your state. Every year there are students who qualify for grant awards but who never get them because their applications arrive either late or incomplete. Don't be one of these poor souls!

Financial Need and Grants

When most people think of grants, need-based grants are what come to mind. "Need," of course, might refer to your "official financial" need, as determined by the results of your FAFSA. It might also refer to some other standardized definition of need, as set by the administrators or donor of the grant.

At any time during the year, if one of your parents loses a job or your family experiences a reduction in income that results in a significant change in your financial circumstances, you should report that information to your college's financial aid office. Depending on the situation, that information may affect your grant eligibility.

Federal and state need-based grants are based on very specific formulas. To put it simply, you will either qualify for a certain grant or you will not, depending upon the awarding criteria for that particular grant. For example, in the 2004–2005 academic year, full-time undergraduate students qualified for a Pell grant if their expected family contributions were $3,851 or less and their cost of attendance was at least $3,900. The amount of the Pell grant ranged from $400 to $4,050, depending on enrollment status (number of credits taken), the applicant's specific expected family contribution, and the school's cost of attendance. Federal and state regulations regarding grants do not allow compassionate financial aid administrators to just give you a grant because you really want or need one. You either fit the requirements, or you don't.

Administrators can, however, use their own professional judgment to alter some of your input data in the FAFSA formula and then recalculate the amount of your expected family contribution. After they do this, you may qualify for a particular grant that you were ineligible for in the beginning. You would need to have very specific and unusual circumstances for the grant administrator to even consider doing this for you. As mentioned earlier, unusually high medical expenses, a parent's loss of a job, or the death of a parent are all examples of the kind of special circumstances that would give you leeway with some administrators, according to their institution's policies regarding professional judgment. If you have special circumstances, you should call or write a letter to the financial aid office to explain your situation. Just remember, these must be extraordinary circumstances in order to be considered for professional judgment.

If you are a parent who is eligible to file a 1040A or 1040EZ federal tax form with the same tax benefits as filing a 1040, then you should choose to file with the A or EZ version. If you file with one of the shorter forms, the levels of adjusted gross income result in a slightly lower EFC calculation, which may help you with grant eligibility.

Federal Grants

There are two kinds of federal grants—the federal Pell grant and the federal Supplemental Educational Opportunity Grant (also referred to as the FSEOG). The only application needed for these two federal grants is the FAFSA. The FAFSA is discussed in detail in Chapter 5.

Federal Pell Grants

These awards go to students with the greatest financial need (meaning the lowest expected family contributions). Financial aid administrators award Pell grants based on the U.S. Department of Education's charts for a given academic year. The Pell grant award is considered an entitlement, which means that in a given year, every student who qualifies for it can get it. Congress sets the levels of spending for this program. For the academic year 2004–2005, a student can be eligible to receive as much as $4,050. In addition to a student's EFC, enrollment status and the cost of education at the particular institution are also factors in determining the amount of the award.

To be eligible for federal student aid programs, including Pell and FSEOG, students must make satisfactory academic progress. Every institution is required to have a policy outlining satisfactory academic progress that includes quality and quantity (number of credits taken and grades earned). The institution's policy may include the requirement of a probationary semester if the student does fall below one of the required levels.

Federal Supplemental Educational Opportunity Grant (FSEOG)

FSEOG awards supplement the Pell grant for a number of students. The FSEOG program is not an entitlement program, so not all Pell grant students will be able to get a FSEOG. Instead, FSEOG is considered a "campus-based" program, which means that a sum of money is given to each institution on an annual basis. The college or university is then able to award the money according to its own policy. Nevertheless, there are certain guidelines that institutions are required to follow in awarding this money.

FSEOG money must go to the most exceptionally needy students first, which usually means those students who are eligible for a Pell grant. Schools have different policies in place to be sure this happens. For instance, some institutions award FSEOG funds only to the neediest half of their Pell grant recipients. Other institutions might award FSEOG money to all their Pell grant recipients on a simple first-come, first-serve basis—so be sure to file your FAFSA ahead of the deadline! Generally, an institution's students have a lot more collective financial need than the FSEOG allocation is able to cover, so the money can end up getting spread pretty thin. It can even run out before all the students who need help get it.

State Grants

Some states offer very generous grant programs for residents who are attending, or who plan to attend, a college in their home state. Some state grants (a good portion of them) are even allowed to follow a student who chooses to attend college in a neighboring state, as long as the two states have reached a reciprocal agreement regarding their respective grant programs.

Colleges and universities do not have to decide who receives Pell grants and how much each student receives. Institutions that participate in federal student aid (FSA) programs must award Pell grants for the U.S. Department of Education according to FSA formulas that determine which students are eligible and how much each student receives.

State Requirements

Some states only require that you complete the FAFSA to apply for one of their grants. However, other states may request an additional form or some other kind of supplemental information (such as a copy of the student's and parents' tax returns for the prior fiscal year) in order to determine a student's eligibility for a grant. Do not ignore any requests for additional information that come from your state's higher education agency. Releasing this information will not hurt you. Also, they will not keep sending you additional requests if you fail to respond. No reply from you, no money from them! It's that simple.

Where to Find State Grants

To find out about what state grants are available in your state and the application requirements, go online to the federal government's education Web site at *www.ed.gov* and search for EROD (the Education Resource Organizations Directory). EROD lists the name and address of every state's higher education agency, along with its telephone and fax numbers, Web site, and e-mail address.

Institutions might not automatically consider for grants you if you do not follow financial aid application procedures to the letter. Not everyone needs or even wants grant assistance. If you don't complete the necessary forms, they will assume that you are just not interested.

Institutional Grants

As mentioned before, some colleges and universities have endowed funds that are available to offer grant assistance to qualifying students. These institutional grants might be need-based, or they might be aimed at students with special talents or other qualifying factors. Make sure you know what applications are required to apply for grants at each institution you are considering. For example, if you apply for admission to five schools, it would not be unusual for three of them to require only the FAFSA, while one requires the CSS profile in addition to the FAFSA with the other requiring the FAFSA, CSS profile, and an additional institutional application.

What Are Institutional Grants Worth?

You might be surprised at how much money you can be awarded through one of your institution's need-based grant programs. Some institutions award as much as 60 percent or more of a student's financial need in institutional grant money. (Once again, need is considered the cost of attendance minus the expected family contribution calculated from the FAFSA.) Different institutions call this type of need-based grant by different names. For example, you might hear terms like "college grant," "presidential grant," or "education award." It doesn't matter what the aid is called—find out what an institution offers in need-based grants, and apply for it!

Some colleges and universities offer grants from their institutional funds based on things other than financial need. If there is a grant available for musical talent and you excel in that area, be sure to apply. Do not be afraid to ask about possibilities for grants at each school based on such things as talents, abilities, or religious affiliation.

When dealing with institutional grants, you should remember that you will have to apply for need-based aid each year (unlike scholarships, which have a set duration and amount of award). In other words, if you get a certain grant for one academic year, you are not assured of receiving the same grant in subsequent years. If your family's income and asset information increases or decreases, or the number of college students in your household changes, you could get more or less need-based grant assistance in future years. For grants that are not based on need, there also might be another application process. Find out in advance, and make sure you do not accidentally turn a renewable grant into a one-shot deal because you failed to follow up.

Where to Find Institutional Grants

Obviously, you should check with the financial aid office at each school you are interested in to find out about the scholarship and grant possibilities they offer from their own funds. It is also a good idea to check with faculty members—the department secretary would be a good start—in your major or minor. Sometimes a specific academic department, instead of by the school's financial aid office, awards certain institutional scholarships or grants. Make an effort to make your professors aware that you are interested in being considered for anything they have to offer. If you have a particular award in mind, it would not hurt to let them know exactly what you are interested in. This is especially important after you have been in college for a year or two and have gotten to know some of your professors well. If they know you, and your academic abilities are strong, they are more likely to recommend you for departmental grants.

You might also check with the college's study abroad or internship office to find out if there are any grants available for certain types of programs. Sometimes alumni or other individual donors set up grants to assist a student with some type of experiential learning (such as a summer study-abroad course for foreign language). This might not help you to pay your regular tuition bills, but it just might help pay for something else worthwhile, such as internship expenses or a part of your off-campus costs.

Certain organizations even hand out grants that cover a student's books or other educational expenses aside from tuition. Always keep a vigilant lookout for any programs like this!

Private Grants

Unlike scholarships, which can be easily found on the Web or through your school, private grants can be obscure, even a real pain in the neck to find. However, you must once again put on your investigator's hat (to do some extra digging around in style). Private grants are a lot like walls in a pitch-dark house—you cannot see them, and you have no idea how to find them, but if you walk around long enough, you'll run into one. Look for scholarships and grant opportunities from private companies as well as nonprofit organizations. For example, here are a few of the private grants available to students: the Princess Grace Dance Grant, the Double Take Sweepstakes, and the ASCAP Foundation Morton Gould Young Composer Award (just to name a few). These grants are described in the following sections to give you an idea of what private foundations can offer. If you don't qualify for any of these, be patient and keep searching—you'll find plenty more options out there.

The Princess Grace Dance Grant

The Princess Grace Dance Grant is a national program whose goal is to find up-and-coming artists in dance, theater, and film, and then give them the assistance they need to realize their goals. The program awards scholarships, grants, and fellowships to applicants deemed both eligible and the most worthy. In order to be eligible, applicants are required to be citizens or permanent resident aliens of the United States. Funds are awarded based upon artistic ability as demonstrated through an applicant's work, creative potential, and the value of the aid to the applicant's artistic growth.

Dance scholarships are available for students with at least a year of formal dance training, undergraduate instruction, or graduate work with a nonprofit organization (but have danced for a nonprofit dance group for no more than five years). Applicants for these funds must be nominated by either the school's dean or department chair. Fellowship applicants must also be nominated by the artistic director.

The federal government requires that you report all sources of financial aid to the financial aid office of your college or university. If you start receiving any outside scholarships after your aid has been determined, they must be incorporated into your current financial aid package.

DoubleTake Sweepstakes

If you are considering a private student loan, investigate the benefits and incentives associated with your loan options. Doing so could win you some scholarship or grant money. An example of an innovative program associated with student loans in the 2004–2005 academic year is the Educaid DoubleTake Scholarship Sweepstakes. In this program, anyone who applies for a loan through Educaid is automatically eligible to receive an award of up to $2,500. This money can be used to cover your own college education costs, or (for parents) those of your student.

Another great thing about this program is that it benefits more than the student or parent—the school also gets a little help. All recipients of the DoubleTake Scholarship Sweepstakes get an additional award of up to $2,500 to be added to their accredited college's respective scholarship funds or financial aid programs. Twenty-four awards are given out in the DoubleTake Scholarship Sweepstakes each year. To find out more or apply for the program, visit the official Educaid Web site (*www.educaid.com*).

Young Composer Award

Morton Gould was president of the American Society of Composers, Authors, and Publishers (a group commonly known as ASCAP) and of the ASCAP Foundation from 1986 until 1994. Considered a very talented composer, Gould won a Pulitzer Prize for his work. ASCAP continues to pay reverence to Gould's passion for the arts and his lifelong commitment to the development of fledgling creators by hosting the annual ASCAP Foundation's Young Composer Awards.

This is a private grant given in Gould's memory. Winners divide a total purse of over $30,000, and funds are distributed in the form of ASCAP Foundation Awards. Original music of any style will be considered for award of these grants. However, work is ineligible if it was previously submitted or if it earned any form of award from any other national competition. Musical arrangements are also deemed ineligible for consideration.

To be considered for this award, candidates must provide a completed application form along with one reproduction of a manuscript or score, a list of biographical information that includes prior academic programs completed in music, and a short description of personal background that describes experience and a current list of compositions performed.

Grants for Graduate Students

For the most part, this book addresses financial aid issues that pertain to the undergraduate student; however, grants are common at the graduate level. Graduate level grants are given to students in order to help them perform research to complete a particular project, and sometimes they even include allotments for housing as well as commuting or other travel expenses. Other common "grant-type" awards found at the graduate level are fellowships and assistantships, which typically cover a graduate student's living expenses or provide a tuition waiver in exchange for a research or teaching obligation. An undergraduate student might also find these opportunities, but they are usually offered at the graduate level.

Check out information on all kinds of graduate schools at the Grad Profiles Web site (*www.gradprofiles.com*). At this site, you will be able to find out more specific information about a number of grad schools as well as what kind of financial aid possibilities exist at each of them.

Princess Grace Film and Theater Awards

The Princess Grace Film Scholarships are available to undergraduate seniors or graduate students so that they may complete their thesis projects. Every year, the Princess Grace Foundation sends out invitations to accredited film schools, asking that they nominate applicants. Film applications are usually mailed around the month of March to these invited schools. Contact the Princess Grace Foundation find out if your school is eligible to make nominations.

The Princess Grace Foundation also awards theater scholarships. These are awarded to students in their final year of study (whether in a graduate or undergraduate program) in the areas of acting, scene design, stage technology, film direction, and/or costume design. Applicants for these awards must be nominated either by one the school's deans or by a department chair. Theater apprenticeships/fellowships are meant to recognize individuals who have worked with an organization for no more than five years and who have received the artistic director's nomination.

State Programs

Some states even have tuition grants that can be awarded to students who qualify for the program to help pay for continuing education in a graduate program. A good example of one of these state programs is the New York State Tuition Assistance Program. This state-funded program awards qualified, graduate-level college students between $75 and $550 per year, depending upon the availability of funds as well as the demonstrated financial need of student applicants.

Health Professionals

Another useful Web site with pertinent information on graduate student financial aid opportunities for those with a focus of study in a health profession (whether you are a graduate or undergraduate student) may be found at *http://bhpr.hrsa.gov*. This site is sponsored by the U.S. Department of Health and Human Services. A number of loans and scholarships can also be found on the site.

Humanities Majors

For academically qualified students interested in pursuing a master's or doctorate degree in the arts, humanities, or social sciences, the Jacob K. Javits Fellowship Program (offered through the U.S. Department of Education) is a great opportunity. The program funds a portion of the student's tuition and fees and also includes a cash stipend (as much as $30,000!). Demonstrated financial need is among the award criteria.

The U.S. Environmental Protection Agency sponsors a good Web site with information on financial aid opportunities for students in environmental majors (in both graduate and undergraduate programs). Check out *www.epa.gov* for information on grants, research associate positions, paid training opportunities, and fellowships.

Heads Up, Law Students!

Those who plan to pursue graduate studies as law students might be very interested to know that the American Bar Association offers a renewable annual scholarship for minority law students in the amount of $5,000 a year.

Demonstrated financial need, however, is part of what determines the award recipients (meaning it may not be exclusively awarded to minorities). Law students should check with their state and county bar associations to find out if scholarships are available to local residents. Many banks also offer special low-interest loans specifically to those pursuing occupations in medicine, law, business, and a number of other profession graduate-level programs.

Other Graduate Aid Examples

The American Association of University Women offers a wide range of grants and fellowships to women enrolled in graduate-level degree programs—to find out more, visit the association's Web site at *www.aauw.org*. The National Black MBA Association offers some a number of substantial scholarships to qualified minority graduate-level students. The requirements for most (if not all) of these scholarships include focused study in a field pertinent to an MBA. To find out more, please visit the association's Web site at *www.nbmbaa.org*.

Chapter 9

Searching for Free Money

It may be true that the best things in life are free. Unfortunately, the things you *need* almost always come at some cost. In fact, necessary items are the most expensive. If you cannot afford them on your own, you will have to get money from somewhere else. As a student, if you find that you have get money from a source other than a personal bank account, it is ideal to get it from somewhere that does not expect to be paid back . . . ever.

Understanding "Free Money"

"Free money" does not mean money that magically rains down from the sky and lands in your lap like a gift from the heavens as you drive off to college. The "free" part of "free money" means that this is money you do not have to pay back to anyone, ever. That is undoubtedly the best part about "free money"—no interest, no regret, and no financial backfiring.

Unfortunately, prospective college students often make the mistake of thinking that just because the money is free, it will be easier to get and all they have to do is apply for it. In fact, getting these funds may not be not as easy as you think. Students who want to receive the benefits of free-and-clear financial aid will have to do a lot of work and searching to locate and be granted any form of free money.

Even finding a source of free money doesn't guarantee that you will get it—you still may have to fulfill obligations such as grades, volunteerism, or participation in certain activities. Once you find something you qualify for, you still have to apply and be accepted.

Finding This So-Called "Free Money"

You've already learned a great deal about scholarships and grants. Free money usually comes in one of these two forms; however, you might also find it under another name, such as a reduction, rebate, or waiver of an educational expense that you otherwise would have had to pay.

Working hard at getting good grades in high school and getting involved in activities, as mentioned in Chapter 1, is likely to help you receive all the free money you will need to pay your way at some colleges, but only if you are extremely diligent in searching for it. While researching and visiting the different colleges and universities you are interested in, you and your parents should make it a point to find out exactly what kind of and how many scholarships or other opportunities are available, what amounts they are available in, and how and when to apply for them.

A financial aid administrator can assist families in applying for federal, state, and institutional aid, but don't make the mistake of stopping your search for free money there. Internet searches can be another good way for parents and students to locate payback-free money. Do searches for grants and scholarships on different search engines.

Sign up for scholarship searches, but avoid those that require a fee for the service. Some well-known and reputable scholarship search Web sites are: *www.fastweb.com,* *www.srnexpress.com,* *www.collegenet.com,* and *www.collegeboard.com* (through the "For Students" link).

Of course, private sources of aid may also be available to students through their high school, community, or local businesses. These unique opportunities can be found in your particular geographic area, and they are not usually advertised nationally. Keep your eyes and ears open for any advertisements or notices of local financial aid resources that may be available only in your area. Programs offered by your state are another possible source of free grant or scholarship assistance. (Find more information on in-state programs on page 117.)

How Do I Get Free Money?

At some colleges, all you need to do to be considered for scholarship awards is simply complete the application for admission. At other schools, however, more may be required—such as multiple applications, additional information, or essays. Students and parents should do their best to find out what kind of aid is offered at a school, what is required to get it, and when pertinent information is required. We cannot stress this enough—be sure that grant and scholarship deadlines are not missed. Few donors of student financial aid are even willing to accept late applications, and if they do accept them, applicant tardiness is sometimes marked on the application.

To Find Free Money, Use Your SEAT

Some students are pretty successful at searching for scholarships, grants, and other free-money opportunities on the Internet. Others, however, spend hours upon hours searching and applying just to get a whole lot of nothing in return. How can some students generate cash for college so easily while others just end up wasting their time? The answer is simple—they knew how to use a SEAT. This handy little acronym refers to the four basic elements to a successful pursuit of free money for college—"Scores, Effort, Appearance, and Timing."

In addition to Internet searches, free-money resources include any number of useful books on scholarship and grant opportunities that can be purchased at your local bookstore. One or two of these books can give you a lot of leads. If you don't want to buy your own copies, you can borrow them from most high school guidance offices and public libraries.

Scores Equal Credentials

A student who scores a 1500 on the SATs certainly has a better chance at winning a scholarship than a student who scored half that does. The higher your scores, the more scholarship and grant opportunities you are eligible to apply for. You can visualize your financial-aid opportunities as an upside-down pyramid—the higher you get, the more money is available. Your good grades and test scores will move you up toward this wider range of aid possibilities. For example, scholarships may be allotted for students who are in the top 5 percent of their high school graduating class, with SAT scores of at least 1300 and a minimum grade point average of 3.6 or higher on a 4.0 scale. A student with strong academic credentials will likely be eligible scholarships like these, while a student with poorer scores will have fewer options to choose from.

Keep in mind that even if you are a higher-scoring student, if you fail to get your application in the mail on time, or choose not to make the effort, someone who is better organized and more ambitious might get it instead (despite their lower scores).

E is for Effort

If you are not exactly a high-scoring test taker, this is not a reason for panic. There are plenty of other kinds of free money that are not based solely upon a student's academic merit. Maybe you didn't get the most stellar score on the SAT. You will still find opportunities to qualify for free money. For instance, some programs are based on nonscholastic factors such as gender, race, ethnicity, financial need, hobbies, volunteerism, special needs, or a parent's vocation or employer. Your credentials and background might help you qualify for free money that is unavailable to a so-called "smarter" student. You just need to put in the time and effort to find these opportunities and take advantage of them.

Don't fool yourself by thinking that just because you took several hours to search and apply for a couple of free money opportunities, you are a shoe-in to get at least one of them. Success is going to take a *lot* of effort. Applying for free money is a lot like applying for a job—sometimes it takes quite a few tries before you get a positive response.

Your search for free money can fit into three categories: government aid, institutional aid, and aid from other sources. Take the initiative in all three areas. Work with an institution's financial aid office to apply for all the government and institutional aid you possibly can. Use some private-investigator skills, the Internet, or even old-fashioned resources like your local public library to find financial aid from all other sources.

Try to complete as much of your search as possible before you graduate from high school (if that's still possible). No matter how much searching you did in high school, however, you should continue this search throughout college. New opportunities become available all the time, and you do not want to miss out on them. Understand that you are going to have to set aside time to put some *effort* into this. Just think of the Internet search for free money as good practice for all of the research and writing that you will have to do when college time finally arrives.

It's especially important that you keep track of your efforts, what sites you visit, and what scholarships you apply for. By staying organized, you will not waste time duplicating your work unnecessarily by applying to scholarships multiple times just because you forgot which ones you already applied for. You might even be able to modify one essay to fit another application—if you were organized enough to save the original essays and can remember what you named the file (or where you hid the hard copies).

Appearance—First Impressions Don't Happen Twice

It is not just what you say that matters but how you say it. Although it is possible to be a bit too boastful, a student has more to fear from being too modest when filling out applications for free money. Administrators may have to read through hundreds, even thousands, of applications before deciding on who is awarded funding. You want your application to be more than a fair and honest presentation of who you are and what you're about—you also want it to stand apart from everyone else's application.

Timing Is Everything

Some students wait until after they graduate from high school to begin searching for free money. High school seniors are so busy with all kinds of time-consuming things like homework, school activities, applying to colleges, and the myriad social activities that take place during the year. College is an entire year away, after all, and it just does not seem reasonable to get all stressed out about money so far in advance.

These students plan to wait until they have a little more free time and all their high school activities are finally over. The bad news is that by that time, most opportunities for free money have already passed them by. That's because deadlines and application due dates fall at some point during the year prior to when the student will begin college—in other words, the student's senior year of high school. This means that by the time he or she graduates from high school, the deadline for application is already long passed.

The ideal mode of action is to start investigating scholarship opportunities in the student's junior year of high school (even freshman and sophomore years are not too early). This way, you already know the deadline dates in advance and can mark them down on your senior timeline (whatever that is). You might even be able to do some of the more time-consuming work in advance (such as writing essays).

In some instances, your search for free money can include a waiver of the admissions application fee. Many institutions offer an application fee waiver if you apply for admission by a certain date, attend certain campus visit programs, or schedule an on-campus interview and tour.

Remember, free money is not just outside scholarship money. Grant money is free money, too. Students and parents should make sure to complete the FAFSA by the earliest required deadline and complete any additional forms that are needed before the deadline. You could needlessly miss out on a lot of free money opportunities if you miss a deadline due to bad timing.

Free Money from In-State Programs

Many states have specific programs to help students pay for a college education. Pennsylvania, for example, has the Temporary Assistance for Needy Families (TANF) education award program. This program is designed to help pay for the educational expenses of certain financially needy students. In this program, and others like it, funds are based on financial need to eligible undergraduate students enrolled at least half-time in an approved college or career school.

Another special program, also in Pennsylvania, is the New Economy Technology Scholarship Program. This program is for residents who plan to attend an in-state college or university and major in a scientific, technological, or computer-based field of study. The award can be as much as $9,000 (divided up into annual $3,000 increments over a span of three years).

FACT

Many states have scholarship programs open specifically to residents of that state. If you are considering any colleges within your home state, be sure to check out these opportunities. The best source for information is your state's higher education agency. Check the blue pages of your telephone book, where all government offices are listed, or do a Web search for find the agency's site.

Recipients of Pennsylvania's New Economy Technology Scholarship Program must maintain a certain grade point average while attending school, complete an internship before they graduate, and agree to work in the state of Pennsylvania after graduation for no less than one year for every year of school they received assistance. That may sound like quite a lot of obligation. However, $9,000 is quite a lot of money. To some students, the potential benefits of a high-tech education are well worth the cost of a few extra years working and living in their home state.

The Robert C. Byrd Honors Scholarship Program

All states, as well as the District of Columbia and Puerto Rico, either participate in the Robert C. Byrd Honors Scholarship Program or have a similar program. The Byrd program is federally funded and state administered. It offers merit-based scholarships to outstanding high school seniors who have already been accepted to an institution of higher education. The Byrd program rewards students for academic excellence in high school and encourages high school seniors to continue their education. The federal government allocates the funding for each state annually, which determines the amounts of scholarship awards. The average award is $1,500 per year, renewable, for up to four years.

QUESTION?

Should I pay someone to help me find financial aid?
NO! High school guidance counselors, college admissions representatives, and financial aid administrators are more than able to answer any questions you may have. Free help is also available from the U.S. Department of Education and elsewhere on the Web. (See Appendix B of this book for plenty of good resources.)

Eligibility for the Byrd Program

In order to be eligible for consideration in the Robert C. Byrd Honors Scholarship Program, students must meet the following criteria:

- Be a high school graduate in the same academic year as the award is made.
- Already be accepted for enrollment at a "Byrd-eligible" college.
- Be a U.S. citizen or able to provide evidence of permanent U.S. residency.
- Be a legal resident of the state in which the student is applying.
- Be enrolled full-time, following high school graduation, at a college in the United States.

Applicants must also submit a copy of an application and letter of acceptance from an eligible college. However, a submitted letter of acceptance is not required from the school the student actually attends.

Further Requirements

In order to receive an award from the Byrd program or others like it, as a student, you must apply directly to your state's higher education agency. You must also be renew your applications annually. You are usually expected to meet or surpass several educational requirements and continuous criteria. Parents and students alike should keep in mind that all of these eligibility requirements must also continue to be met for as long as the student has the scholarship. In the case of the Byrd program, these requirements include the following:

- Must be ranked in the top 5 percent of high school graduating class. If the applying student's graduating class consisted of 60 or less graduating seniors, student must hold a class ranking of 1, 2, or 3.
- Transcript must show a cumulative grade point average of 3.50 or above, scored on a 4.00 (unweighted) scale.
- Minimum SAT score of 1150 (combined verbal and math), or minimum ACT composite score of 25 or above, or minimum completed GED with a score of 355 or above. (TOEFL scores are not accepted for consideration in the Byrd program.)

Take note that the Robert C. Byrd Honors Scholarship Program does not make awards to students who plan to attend a college in another country. Award of these scholarships, as well as many others similar to them, are also very much dependent upon the availability of federally based college funding. States receive money for this program from the federal government, and each state's allocation varies from year to year. States generally select winners from all qualified applicants through a lottery system. Check with your state agency for more information on its selection process.

Guard your social security number and bank information! Identity theft is a growing problem in the United States. Before you include it, be sure that this information will be protected if it is needed on a scholarship or grant application.

In-State Versus Out-of-State Students

Some institutions have different costs for in-state and out-of-state students. Does this mean that prospective students should choose an in-state school over an out-of-state school just to save some money? Maybe—but then again, maybe not. Perhaps the out-of-state school is much better suited to your needs and goals. If so, it's worth every penny and more of the added expense. Don't decide too hastily whether a college or university in your home state is the right school. In fact, there are several types of aid that may make an out-of-state school affordable after all.

Scholarships for Out-of-State Students

An institution may offer scholarships to out-of-state students that could even out the increased cost of tuition. Also, you or your student might even be able to piece together enough "free money" of your own to make attendance at an out-of-state school within the realm of affordability.

The Federal Trade Commission's Web site provides information about scholarship scams as well as tips to help keep consumers from getting ripped off by any of these illegal schemes. Visit *www.ftc.gov,* and use the "Consumer Information" link to find out more.

Out-of-State Tuition Waivers

Some states use tuition waivers as a way of attracting students to certain schools. Basically, all state universities are part of a state-run higher education system. One big-name university is usually the most popular and best known—it is the so-called "flagship" college in the state. Another college that is part of that same state-run system might have just as many opportunities and programs, but because it doesn't have the same prestige, it is hard for the school to draw as many students.

This is where the waivers come in. The less-popular university may decide to waive extra tuition and other added fees for out-of-state students who meet the qualifications for the honors program. As an out-of-state student, you would pay the same lower rate of tuition as an in-state student. If you qualify, this is most certainly a viable option, even if you had originally planned to spend the first two years at community college in order to graduate at an out-of-state school.

Community College First?

Guidance counselors often encourage their students to spend the first couple of years of their higher education at a lower cost, local community college, and then transfer later to one of the state's big-name universities. Understandably, they are simply trying to save students and their parents some money. There is no fault in this, but sometimes guidance counselors do their students a disservice by not providing them with alternate plans of action.

Community college is much better than no college at all. There is no shame in having a degree from a technical training program, a vocational school, or a community college. The most important thing, when it comes down to it, is that you have a degree in the first place (no matter where it may be from).

There is no disputing that the "community college first" method has the potential to save students, as well as their parents, a substantial amount of money. However, if you're thinking along these lines, you and your parents must also consider how much quality you are going to sacrifice in your college experience. In the quest to save money, it might be better in the long run to look into the tuition waiver option.

Textbook Savvy—Save Money, and Get Some Back

Let's face it. Unless the professor cuts students a break and makes the textbook optional, you are going to have to buy books for all the classes you take. Textbooks are a rough subject for many college students—mainly because they are so expensive to buy and do not return much in the way of cash when you sell them back. Although textbook costs are notoriously high, there are a few things you can to do to save a little money.

In a way, saving money on buying and selling textbooks is another way to create our favorite kind of money—the free kind. The less you have to spend on textbooks, the less you have to beg or borrow from someone or somewhere else. This also translates into extra money for you (or your family) to spend on other expenses—maybe even a summer road trip or a spring break cruise. Or, better yet, a slushie every now and then! With that said, here are a few textbook-buying tips.

Buy Them Used

First of all, used versions of textbooks are priced at significant reductions, sometimes costing as little as half the cost of a new book. As a result, the cheaper used textbooks often end up selling like hotcakes, so be sure to get to the bookstore early so you don't miss out on a good opportunity to save.

Oftentimes, you can still find used versions of textbooks in off-campus bookstores even after the campus store sells out. Unfortunately, they will likely not be as cheap as those you could have found on-campus. However, a more expensive used textbook from the off-campus bookstore is probably still cheaper than a new version that you buy from anywhere else.

Keep your eyes out for other options as well. Some students try to sell their books directly to other students rather than back to the bookstore. Watch for flyers listing such offers. You also may want to find out if your friends or dorm mates took any of your courses last semester. They might still have a book or two lying around and be willing to part with them for a little cash.

Share and Share Alike

There is no shame in sharing a book with one or more of your classmates. However, this is only a good idea if you know the student(s) you plan to share the book with fairly well. You should also make absolutely certain that you and this person will be good at sharing. Both of you must be able to have access to the book when you need it, and you have to respect one another enough to work around schedule conflicts.

Consider the course schedule carefully, and decide if there is really enough time between assignments to make this option feasible. You also need to think about your respective living situations. (Hand-offs will be much easier if you live down the hall from each other than if one of you lives in a separate dorm or even off campus.)

Buy Online

In any case, you always have the option of ordering your textbooks online. The discount Web site *www.half.com* (and other such textbook Web sites) usually have good deals on new and used textbooks.

FACT

Once you know which textbooks are required for the courses you are taking each semester, go to the college bookstore as soon as humanly possible. There may be some used versions of certain required books still available, which will save you from having to pay full price (sometimes a hefty sum).

Be careful with your timing, though. Don't wait until a week after the start of the semester to order your textbooks online. Commonly, books that are purchased online are shipped via the standard media option, which means they make it to their destinations in about four to fourteen days. Be sure you are prepared to wait that long and that you will still be able to complete your assignments on time. Of course, you always have the option of paying a little more so they will ship a few days faster.

You Bought 'Em Online . . . Now Sell 'Em Online

Usually, you can sell your textbooks to someone else online in the same way you bought them. You can get a quite a bit more for them this way than the pittance you're likely to get selling them back to the college bookstore.

The best time to sell your books online is just before the beginning of the next semester. This means you will have to suppress the desire for immediate gratification that comes with selling your textbooks at the campus bookstore for cash in hand. True, that method does put money into your pocket immediately, and it is better than nothing, but it is also a bit of a scam. Sell a whole semester's books, which cost you $500 at the beginning of the semester, and you're lucky to walk away $100 in your pocket. It doesn't help that the bookstore will turn around and sell those books for twice as much—sometimes as much as ten times more—than what they just paid you.

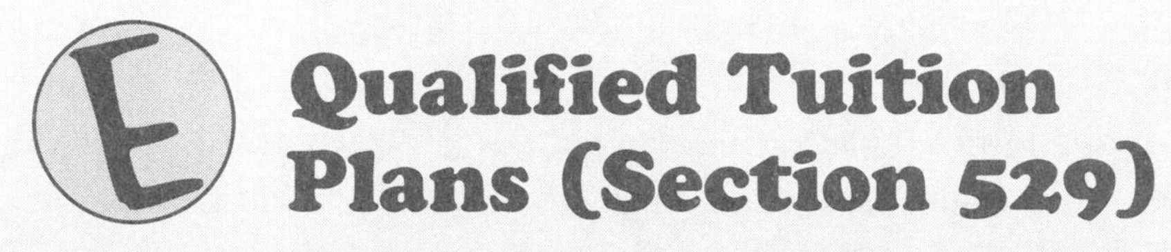

Chapter 10

Qualified Tuition Plans (Section 529)

Qualified tuition plans, or Section 529 plans, as they are also known, are a very good tool for families to use in meeting the financial part of their college goals for their children. Section 529 plans are savings plans operated by state governments (or eligible educational institutions). They are usually managed by established investment companies. They can be set up to prepay tuition or contribute to a current or future student's education. One of the best factors of 529 plans is that as you save up college money, you also get some nice tax exemptions.

Two Types of 529 Plans

The savings plans known as Section 529 plans are set up under the Internal Revenue Code Section 529 (hence the name) as part of the 2001 Tax Relief Act. There are two main types of Section 529 plans—prepaid tuition plans and college savings plans. When these plans were first implemented, many states offered the prepaid tuition option to their residents. Unfortunately, the average rate of increase for college tuition was greater than the growth rate of funds in these plans. Because the prepaid plan couldn't keep up with these tuition increases, states began to move away from this option.

These days, most Section 529 plans are college savings plans, which are very similar to just about any other type of investment vehicle. You put your money into the plan and (hopefully) watch it start to grow. Section 529 plans may not achieve the highest of returns on your invested money; on the plus side, however, the tax benefits are quite substantial.

Advantages of College Savings Plans

In terms of the FAFSA and other applications for financial aid, college savings plans are also treated with a certain amount of favor. Prepaid tuition plans are counted as a resource in the student's financial aid package (and, therefore, might bring the total high enough to disqualify the student for certain other types of financial aid). A college savings plan, on the other hand, is counted as an asset of the account holder—usually the parent. Consequently, the funds are not considered a part of a student's financial aid package, even though they are applied to education costs. This helps keep the total of the financial aid package low enough so that the student might still qualify for certain other types of aid. Assets, including a college savings plan, are included in the EFC calculation, but not at 100 percent.

Each of the fifty states is currently participating in Section 529 plans for college tuition assistance. This means that no matter where you live or attend school, they are there to be found.

A college savings plan may provide you with more options than a prepaid tuition plan because it gives you greater flexibility in your choice of colleges. This is a significant advantage when you consider that a savings plan can start ten to fifteen years (sometimes more) before the college selection process is actually underway.

Common Traits of Section 529 Plans

No matter which type of Section 529 plan you end up with, there are some important features you should know about. It is always good to know as much as you can when it comes to investment planning. If you know what you're getting into, you're less likely to get blindsided later on. Here are some of the basic facts about Section 529 plans:

- Earnings from Section 529 plans are exempt from federal taxes, as are withdrawals used for paying college costs.
- Some states also waive state tax for residents, while others allow deductions on contributions.
- Section 529 plans have generous maximum contribution limits, as much as $250,000 per beneficiary.
- Most states hire investment companies to manage these plans, for maximum investment efficiency and return.
- Funds withdrawn for purposes other than education are subject to a 10-percent penalty and to federal income taxes. (States assess their own penalties.)

Remember that Section 529 plans change depending upon your state of residence. Depending on where you live, some of the above factors may not apply. However, being aware of the most common factors will at least empower you to ask your Section 529 plan provider about which of these traits will apply to your specific situation.

Get the Grandparents Involved!

Section 529 plans are a really good idea for parents who are saving for a child's college education. They also allow for contributions by grandparents and anyone else who wants to help. Saving money now could mean borrowing a lot less money later (which translates into a lot less to be paid back—with interest). With Section 529 plans, grandparents enjoy a tax benefit while providing their grandchildren money to help pay for education.

Section 529 plans have grown into one of the most popular methods for families to start saving for their children's college education. Though these plans may be different from one state to another, they are all exempt from federal income tax, and that could translate into one heck of a contribution to a student's college fund.

Qualified Education Expenses

The money in a Section 529 Plan should be dedicated to paying "qualified education expenses." These expenses include tuition, fees, books, course supplies, room and board, and required course equipment. All of these expenses must be charged by an institution the U.S. Department of Education considers to be eligible for participation. The student must also be enrolled at least half-time at this accredited institution.

No one savings plan is 100-percent perfect for everyone. Before you decide to enroll in any plan, be sure to investigate and weigh all the benefits and risks very carefully. Some of the factors that need to be considered are your level of income, the age of the child, the plan's mandatory fees, and what investment options are available with the plan.

Qualified educational expenses are reduced by any tax-free financial aid the student receives, such as tax-free scholarships, veterans' benefits, Pell grants, employer-provided educational assistance, and other nontaxable forms of educational assistance. The taxable part is based on the difference between the total of the distributions and the adjusted qualified educational expenses. See IRS Publication 970 (available on the Web at *www.irs.gov*) for an explanation of how to determine the amount of qualified educational expenses you have.

Improper Use of Section 529 Plans

Since they were introduced in 1996, thousands of investors have taken advantage of Section 529 plans and the way that contributions to the accounts remain tax-free as they grow. Some people take further advantage of the fact that withdrawals stay free from federal tax as long as the funds are used for education expenses. Section 529 plans were intended to help those who had already stashed away some money for their children's educations, but changes introduced in 2001 have begun to allow many investors to start bending the original rules. Sadly, this has caused a problem for Section 529 plans. They have begun to attract investors who have no intention of using the account to put their children through college.

Not long after the new tax laws of 2001 were put into action, many financial advisers began working out ways for clients to take creative tax advantages from them. As it turned out, Section 529 plans worked really well if used as estate-planning tools because they let the individual investor move quite a bit more money in and out of an estate. Why? After the 2001 tax exemptions, investors could take large amounts of money out of an estate, a lot more than would be normally allowed without incurring some amount of penalty in terms of federal gift taxes.

FACT

Most Section 529 plans are controlled by professional, experienced fund managers. That takes a little bit of the risk out of your investment, especially if you are not investment-savvy or if you do not have enough time to regularly oversee your own investment account. As with all investments, there is no guarantee that you will not end up taking a loss, but at least with a certified fund manager, you'll be less likely to blame yourself if there is one.

Isn't That Illegal?

You would think that taking advantage of educational savings plans with no intention of using the money for education would be illegal, but the sad truth is that it is not. The abovementioned practices, though somewhat unethical, are not considered illegal by the federal government or the Internal Revenue Service. The creative use of Section 529 plans has yet to cause enough of a strain in governmental tax losses to be considered as illegal tax evasion by the IRS. Does that mean it never will? Absolutely not!

Don't Try It!

If you are going to take advantage of a Section 529 plan, be sure you to do so ethically—to pay your student's college tuition. These so-called "creative" investors are in the clear for now because there are currently no laws set down to deter them. They will probably end up getting nailed by the IRS soon enough, especially once old Uncle Sam realizes just how much money he's losing in tax dollars and decides to assemble a federal task force to crack down on Section 529 abusers.

Aside from the possibility of incurring the wrath of the IRS, there are a number of additional risks for investors hoping to shelter their cash in a Section 529 plan. As with most provisions put into action by the 2001 tax reform, most of the changes are set to expire in 2010 unless lawmakers choose to extend the 529 benefits. As the law currently reads, Section 529 account earnings will be taxed at the beneficiary's personal income-tax rate beginning in January 2011.

In addition to tax incentives, Section 529 plans include many other benefits. They can be used for graduate or undergraduate education, the contributions are transferable, contribution limits are high, and there is no age limit on their use.

A bill introduced by Rep. Kenny Hulshof last July proposed making the 2001 changes to Section 529 permanent, canceling out the 2010 expiration. However, Congress has not yet taken action on this proposal.

Tax Benefits of 529s

In addition to the obvious benefit of having money available for your student's college education, Section 529 plans offer tax relief as well. Since it took effect in January of 2002, the Tax Relief Act of 2001 has made Section 529 plans very appealing to many people looking for ways to pay for a college education, whether a child's or their own. Not only are there tax benefits on the account's interest (earnings), there also may be benefits on the money you put into the account (contributions), and money you take out (distributions).

Account Earnings

As of January 1, 2002, all of the earnings from a Section 529 plan account are exempt from federal tax, as long as they are eventually withdrawn for the exclusive use of paying for qualified education expenses. This means that unlike the taxes an investor is normally required to pay on earnings from most types of investments, no taxes are paid on the interest earned by money invested in a Section 529 plan. This holds true unless you withdraw the money for uses other than your student's higher education. Section 529 plan earnings are currently tax-deferred in nearly all states as well, meaning you don't pay taxes on the money as long as it is in a 529. Ask your Section 529 provider if your state gives these tax deferrals.

FACT

The assets in a Section 529 plan belong to the owner of the plan, not to the student beneficiary. If a parent is the owner of the plan, then the assets must be reported on the FAFSA. If someone other than the parent or student is the owner of the plan, it should not be reported as an asset of either the parent or student on the FAFSA.

Contributions and Distributions

A tax break on your Section 529 earnings is only one of the tax advantages that comes with using these plans. Section 529 contributions are not pretaxed, meaning you do not pay state or federal tax on money deposited into an account. Some states also allow you to deduct a set portion of your contributions from state tax. Again, ask your 529 provider about what your state's particular policies are before you start counting on receiving these exemptions.

Generally, distributions (withdrawals) are also tax-free, as long as you don't take out more than the amount equal to the beneficiary's adjusted qualified tuition expenses. Anything above and beyond that amount will be taxed.

Section 529 Plans Are Flexible—Truth or Myth?

Section 529 plans offer a certain amount of flexibility and control—or do they? Unlike a number of investment vehicles, such as custodial accounts (such as the Uniform Gifts to Minors Act) and Coverdell accounts (used to pass money to minors, as explained on page 135), you never surrender your control over a Section 529 plan. This remains true even after the potential beneficiary reaches the age of majority (usually eighteen, but twenty-one in some states).

Beneficiaries Can Change

The owner of the account is the person who contributes the money. The designated beneficiary is the student, current or future, who will receive the benefit. The owner of the account can change the beneficiary after participation in the Section 529 plan begins. You should check with your plan provider to find out how often and when you can change beneficiaries. There is no age limit for the beneficiary, so the funds can be used for undergraduate or graduate education.

The account holder retains sole discretion in deciding when account withdrawals are made and for what purpose. For instance, if your student is awarded a full scholarship or (heaven forbid) decides that college life is "just not meant for him" or "not in her destiny," you can still change the name of your Section 529 beneficiary. Investors are also able to reclaim their funds and return the invested amounts to their private estates. In this case, the withdrawals become subject to federal income taxes as well as a 10-percent tax penalty. What's even better is that you are allowed to start up as many Section 529 accounts as you need and/or want. You would be able to start one account for each child.

In determining federal aid eligibility for a student, the U.S. Department of Education does not currently require financial aid administrators to count as income any distribution from Section 529 plan investments. However, some institutions do count the money as untaxed income of the student when awarding institutional aid, and this may affect the student's institutional grant eligibility.

Plans Vary from State to State

The tax benefits that may be possible if your Section 529 plan is in your state of residence could provide you with an incentive to invest in your home state's plan. Most state plans allow students to attend colleges and universities across the United States, so where you choose to invest should not necessarily restrict your student's choices. When you compare the plans offered by different states, you may find one in another state that is a more attractive investment option (better historic rate of return, lower annual account fees, plan flexibility).

Rollovers from one plan to another are generally allowed. Investors may choose to do a rollover for the same performance reasons you would roll over a retirement plan. If you consider a rollover from one state's plan to another, just be sure to review the originating state's requirements for any restrictions before you make your decision.

Choose Your Own Contributions

There are absolutely no income limits on individual contributors to Section 529 plans, so anyone can contribute, no matter how much money they make. If annual contributions exceed $11,000, gift taxes begin to apply;

the maximum amounts allowed for contribution on behalf of each designated beneficiary vary from state to state. The $11,000 annual contribution ceiling (the point at which federal gift tax begins to apply) is also subject to limitation, as it assumes that the contributor has made no other monetary gifts to the beneficiary in that same tax year.

Keep in mind that you are only granted one gift tax exemption for each of your children. If you start Section 529 plans in two different states, both for the benefit of the same child, then your collective contributions to both accounts would count toward your gift tax exclusion.

In certain situations, an investor can make contribution payments up to five years in advance. An individual contributor can make a single contribution of up to $55,000, and married couples can contribute $110,000 in one lump sum. Beneficiaries are subject to a lifetime limit, which is commonly set in excess of $200,000.

Withdrawals for Whatever You Want?

Most withdrawals from Section 529 college savings plans are exempt from federal taxes. Of course, that's only if the money is used as intended, for qualified educational costs. The owner of the fund *can* withdraw the money for other expenses. However, this incurs a 10-percent penalty, and you also subject those Section 529 funds to federal income taxes. Some plans have a one-year waiting period before any distributions can be made. If the student is close to college age, you may want to check on the distribution requirements of various plans before choosing a particular one.

Some Section 529 plans charge some form of a fee for management or annual account maintenance. The tax advantages that many state plans offer may help to balance the costs for a number of Section 529 plan mandatory fees.

If the Section 529 plan beneficiary receives a scholarship, funds can still be withdrawn without penalty (music to everyone's ears!). However, the withdrawals are only tax exempt up to the total amount of scholarship award. In the event of the beneficiary's death or disability (though hopefully this will not be the case), withdrawals remain tax-exempt. However, your 529 account earnings would be subject to federal income taxes.

Coverdell Accounts Versus Section 529 Plans

Coverdell education savings accounts are not the same as Section 529 plans, but they are another way for you to save money for a college education. Coverdell accounts are trust funds or custodial accounts that must be arranged through a bank or some other IRS-approved financial entity. They are more restrictive than Section 529 plans in some ways. For instance, they impose a small annual contribution limit on the beneficiary, regardless of how many people contribute to the plan.

The Big Minus of Coverdell Accounts

The account contribution limits for a Coverdell account are typically much lower than for Section 529 plans. The set limits on maximum lifetime contributions to Section 529 plans does vary from state to state. However, most limits are in the ballpark of $200,000 to $300,000 per account. This is a pretty hefty sum when you start to consider the measly $2,000 that you are allowed to deposit annually in a Coverdell education savings account.

The Big Plus of Coverdell Accounts

One advantage of Coverdell accounts, however, is that the money can be used for qualified educational expenses for elementary or secondary education in addition to higher education expenses. This means that a Coverdell account could be used to send your student to a good college prep school or private high school, thus getting the student better prepared for the college classroom and improving the chances of acceptance at a top-of-the-list college.

Chapter 11

The Facts About Loans

For most students, paying for college involves taking out some kind of loan. This should not necessarily be considered a bad thing. People borrow money for many big events in their lives—to buy a car, a home, or even start a business. Paying for a college education is one more reason people are willing to take out loans. The important thing is that students and parents become informed as borrowers so they know how to choose the best loan with the lowest interest rate and best payback benefits for their individual situations.

The Stafford Loan

The Stafford loan is a federal loan that is available to undergraduate and graduate college students. This loan is granted completely in the student's name. No co-signer is required or allowed. In order to take out Stafford loan, the student must sign a promissory note—a binding legal document that specifies the obligations that come with the loan.

The Stafford loan can come in one of two forms: a direct Stafford loan or a Federal Family Education Loan (or FFEL) Stafford loan. Basically, these are the same loan, at least from the student's perspective. The difference is that direct Stafford loans are borrowed directly from the college or university, while FFEL Stafford loans are borrowed through a private lending institution (such as a bank or credit union) that participates in the FFEL Stafford loan program. Students must repay the direct Stafford loans to the federal government, but FFEL Stafford loans are repaid to the private lender's designated agency or financial institution.

Stafford Loan Payments

Payment on a Stafford loan is deferred (meaning no payments are due) until after the student graduates or ceases to be at least a half-time student. ("Half time" is a course load of six credit hours, or roughly two courses per semester.) Stafford loans have a variable interest rate, meaning the rate on the loan changes with federal interest rates. Federal interest rates are adjusted on an annual basis, and these adjustments are made on July 1 of each year. The variable interest rate for these loans is capped at 8.5 percent. However, in recent years this rate has been extremely low, staying below 4 percent. As anyone knows who's had to borrow money recently, this is a very good interest rate.

Subsidized Versus Unsubsidized

A student's Stafford loan may be subsidized or unsubsidized. Your qualification for the subsidized or the unsubsidized version will be determined through your FAFSA information. It will also depend upon the other types and amounts of financial aid you already qualify for.

The subsidized Stafford loan is a little better because the government pays off (or "subsidizes") the interest on your loan while you are attending college. Subsidized loans are awarded based upon financial need, and students can get need-based financial aid only up to their official demonstrated need (the school's cost of attendance minus your expected family contribution). If you do not qualify for the subsidized Stafford loan, you can still get an unsubsidized loan, which does not require demonstration of financial need. Interest on unsubsidized Stafford loans starts to accrue from the moment you take out the loan. With the unsubsidized Stafford loan, you have the option of allowing the interest to capitalize (in which case it is added to the principal that you will repay later) or paying off the interest amount in installments on a quarterly basis.

A typical loan-processing timeline for federal Stafford and PLUS loans for fall enrollment would begin when the borrower completes his or her application in May or June. The financial aid office would then certify the loan sometime during the month of August.

How Much Can Be Borrowed?

The amount of a Stafford loan is based upon the student's year in college. For the last several years, Congress has set the annual amount of federal Stafford money that an undergraduate student can borrow at the following limits: $2,625 for freshmen; $3,500 for sophomores; and $5,500 for juniors and seniors. Graduate students can borrow as much as $18,500 per year, regardless of their years in a program. Beyond these basic loan limits, an undergraduate student can borrow as much as an additional $4,000 each year as a freshmen or sophomore student, and an additional $5,000 more each year as a junior or senior. These additional funds are available if the student's parent has been denied a PLUS loan. (You'll find more on PLUS loans on page 142).

Schools are required to divide the award of a Stafford loan into at least two installments, which are typically paid in each semester of the academic year. Funds are distributed to the student, less a small loan-origination fee that is usually deducted each semester. Your direct educational expenses must be paid off before anything else (tuition and fees plus room and board).

Once these have been paid, if any money is left, it may be used toward some of your other, noncomprehensive charges and expenses, such as rent, utilities, books, transportation, and personal expenses.

The Perkins Loan

The Perkins loan is another a federal program for undergraduate and graduate students. As with the Stafford loans, no co-signer is required. Unlike a Stafford loan, the Perkins program is campus-based (as are the Supplemental Educational Opportunity Grant or federal work study programs). The government allocates funds to the institution, and it is the responsibility of the institution to set its own policy regarding who receives a loan. In order to be eligible to receive a Perkins loan, the student must have a certain amount of demonstrated financial need. The Perkins loan places the college or university in the role of lender, so you must pay the money back to your school when the time comes to repay the loan.

If you are a student returning to college, you must not be in default status on any past federal Perkins loans, direct loans, or FFEL Stafford loans. If you are in default status and have not already made satisfactory arrangements for repayment of your past debt, you will not be eligible for any federal financial aid until your default status is resolved.

Perkins loans are subsidized, so no interest accrues as long as you are enrolled in enough courses to qualify as at least a half-time student. When the student finally repays the loan, interest begins to accrue at a set rate of 5 percent.

There are no loan origination fees for a Perkins loan. Loan limits are set at $4,000 for each year of undergraduate study (with no more than $20,000 borrowed total), and $6,000 for each year of graduate study (up to $40,000 total). However, it is very uncommon for educational institutions to have enough money in their budgets to award the federal maximum to their students.

Paying Back Federal Loans

The federal government is more than happy to "give out" money—as long as the person they give it to has to pay the money back. Here is a little note on the way the federal government handles money matters. When it comes to distributing your loan, they will take their sweet time. However, when it comes time for you to pay them, they want their money, and they want it right away. Does this mean federal loans are the wrong way to go? Absolutely not. You just need to know what you are getting into.

FACT

The Student Guide is a free annual publication. Printed by the U.S. Department of Education, it contains valuable information about all kinds of federal financial aid programs, including federal loans, their interest rates, and what your repayment obligations will be. The current publication can be viewed online, and it is also available in print at almost any college or university.

Forgiveness of Federal Loans

In certain cases, if a student meets the right requirements, part of an outstanding Stafford or Perkins loan can be cancelled, which would be absolutely terrific for a recent graduate just starting out in the "real world." For example, as much as $5,000 of a Stafford loan can be forgiven (and never have to be paid) if the student is employed as a full-time teacher for at least five consecutive years at certain elementary or secondary schools whose students come primarily from low-income families. A portion of your Perkins loan might also be forgiven if you serve as a Vista or Peace Corps volunteer or if you are a member of the U.S. Armed Forces and serving in a hostile area.

Can the Whole Loan Be Forgiven?

Again, yes! As much as 100 percent of a Perkins loan can be forgiven if you are a teacher and there is a teacher shortage in your specialty. This may also be an option if you are a full-time nurse or medical technician, a full-time law enforcement officer, or another type of corrections officer.

Parent Loans for Undergraduate Students (PLUS Loans)

PLUS loans are for parents of dependent undergraduate students who are enrolled in college as at least half-time students. Unlike the federal loans we have already discussed, this particular loan is taken in the parent's name instead of the student's. Parent borrowers may be denied approval for PLUS loans, however, if one or both parents have an adverse credit history. Just like the different kinds of Stafford loans, there are FFEL PLUS loans as well as direct PLUS loans. With a direct PLUS program, parents borrow from the federal government through the college or university or through a private lending institution. The college or university participates in either one or the other type of PLUS program. The financial aid office can supply instructions to parents on how to apply.

PLUS Interest Rates

The interest rate for a PLUS loan is variable, and it's quite a bit higher than the rate of a Stafford or Perkins loan. The interest rates of PLUS loans have been capped at 9 percent. However, in recent years, interest on these loans has been much lower than the 9-percent maximum. For example, between July 2003 and July 2004, the PLUS loan interest rate dropped down to a very low 4.22 percent—just a little higher than the ceiling on a Stafford loan!

The Parent Loan for Undergraduate Students (PLUS) is easier to qualify for than some other types of loans because the credit check is based upon federal standards. There are no debt-to-income ratios or credit scoring involved in qualifying for a PLUS loan.

PLUS Advantages and Disadvantages

One of the biggest advantages of having a PLUS loan is that the parent is able to borrow an amount equal to the cost of education (after any other financial aid the student receives is subtracted from this amount). In other words, the parent can borrow up to the expected family contribution on the FAFSA as well as anything that is not covered by certain other types of financial aid.

On the other hand, one big disadvantage of a PLUS loan is that parents have to start paying the loan back a lot earlier. Payment installments must begin within sixty days after the loan has been fully disbursed for one academic year.

FACT

If the parent of a student is denied for a PLUS loan, then the student's educational institution is authorized to automatically award the student as much as $4,000 to $5,000 (for undergraduate freshmen and sophomores or juniors and seniors, respectively) in the form of additional, unsubsidized Stafford loan funds.

Alternative Loan Programs

Alternative loan programs are student educational loans that are funded through either a bank or a credit union. Most of the time, these loans are made in the student's name. Unlike loans such as the Stafford or Perkins, however, a creditworthy co-signer is required for the loan to be approved. Different lending institutions have different loan minimums, maximums, and borrower benefits. With a creditworthy co-signer, most of these loans let the student borrow the total cost of attendance minus any other financial aid that they receive.

Some good examples of alternative loans include the following: Key Alternative Loan through KeyBank, CitiAssist Loan through Citibank, and Resource Loan through PNC Bank. It's a good idea to do a Web search and learn a little bit more about the highlights and downsides of these and other individual loans. These particular loans are popular today, and parents and students across the United States commonly apply for them, but you may also want to investigate similar loans from banks in your local area.

Nellie Mae Foundation EXCEL Loans

There can be benefits to borrowing from alternative sources. Virtually all of them provide applicants with an online application that eliminates the slow process and the nail-biting, bullet-sweating wait of using snail mail or sitting in a bank lobby or loan officer's office. You will usually find out right away if your loan has been approved or denied.

Nellie Mae Foundation's EXCEL Loan is a good example of an alternative student loan that is easy to apply for and that has favorable borrow benefits. Borrower eligibility for a Nellie Mae EXCEL loan is reasonable and straightforward:

- The student, borrower, and/or co-signer must all have proof of a valid Social Security number.
- Of the borrower and the co-signer, at least one of the two must be a U.S. citizen or at least an eligible permanent resident alien.
- Both the borrower and the co-signer must be eighteen years of age or older.
- Any creditworthy individual with an income of $15,000 a year or more is allowed to borrow money on the student's behalf.
- Pre-existing monthly debt obligations are not allowed to exceed 45 percent of monthly income for approval of this loan.
- Students are required to have applied for a federal Stafford loan before they can apply for EXCEL loans, and they must therefore already have a FAFSA on file.

EXCEL loans begin at a minimum of $500. The amount borrowed can be as much as the student's cost of attendance minus other financial aid the student receives. Interest rates can be figured either on a monthly or an annual basis. (Interest is determined using the prime rate, which is set by the U.S. Federal Reserve.) EXCEL loan interest rates are capped at a ceiling of 7 percent, and there are a number of repayment options; a student can pay the interest while enrolled as at least a half-time student or pay the principal as well as interest immediately after the loan has been fully disbursed. For more information on what loans are available, please contact the Nellie Mae Foundation by e-mail or telephone. (See Appendix A for contact information.)

With some alternative loans, it is possible to release the co-signer from the loan obligation once the student has made a certain number of regularly scheduled payments, in full and on time. If you are responsible about making your payments, you can take some of the debt load off your parents—and maybe free them to take out a loan of their own.

Advantages and Disadvantages

An advantage to having an alternative student loan is that your repayment is often deferred until after you have graduated from college. This is because as a student, you are listed as the primary borrower, and it is therefore your responsibility to repay your loan. The bank understands that this probably isn't possible while you are still in school.

On the other hand, one of the disadvantages to having an alternative student loan is that the parent (or whoever your co-signer might have been) is held responsible for paying the loan back if for some reason you do not.

More Loan Options

There are a plethora of student loans in this world, and it would be impossible to list them all in this book. The following sections provide information on a few common types of student loans. Looking into these may help you to find a student loan that is right for your unique situation. Remember that everyone is different, and there is no "umbrella loan" that just works for anybody and everybody. You don't have to settle for what is initially made available to you. Do plenty of checking, and you will be able to sign your loan promissory note with the confidence that comes from knowing your options—and knowing that the loan you finally chose was the very best loan for you.

Student Loan Consolidation

After you graduate, you can consider loan consolidation. Basically, this means taking out one big new loan that combines (or consolidates) all your different federal student loans, with the benefit of giving you one loan payment to worry about. By taking out the consolidation loan, you get to pay off existing loans and then concentrate on repaying the consolidation loan.

Student loan consolidation can significantly lower your monthly payments by extending the duration of your loan's terms, often without incurring any prepayment penalties. Consolidation makes the most sense if you can get a better interest rate than what you're currently paying on your smaller loans. Even with a lower monthly payment, consolidation won't make much sense in the long run if it means paying a lot in interest that you would have otherwise. Currently, interest rates are at historic lows for consolidation loans, and you should be able to find a good rate. Be sure to shop around at your local credit union and banks.

The advantages of a consolidation loan include the convenience of having only one payment (instead of several), possible savings from getting a lower interest rate, and no prepayment penalties or fees. However, be sure to watch out for higher interest rates and/or any tax implications that may be associated with getting a consolidation loan.

The consolidation process is often very easy, and in some cases it can even be done for free. In this context, "free" means that you won't be charged any additional loan-related fees. This does not mean that your new creditor will pay off your loans for free (so don't ask them to!). Believe it or not, some student loan consolidations don't even require a check of your credit history.

What About State Loans?

You could look around for quite a while and not locate any loans funded by state government, though there are some out there. They just seem to be few and far between. Your best bet for locating information on state loans for college students would be at the Web sites of your state's higher education agencies. A Web search for your state government's main information site or a glance at the blue pages of your telephone book (where you can find the listing for any government office) should set you in the right direction.

Home Equity Loans

In recent years, students and parents have been able to enjoy many tax benefits related to their educational and college loans. In addition, parents who own their homes have discovered some attractive tax advantages in taking out a home equity loan. A home equity line of credit is somewhat more flexible than other kinds of loans, though it often comes with a slightly higher interest rate. The loan is for a specific monetary amount based upon the equity in your home. You draw from a line of credit as you need the money, without having to pay interest until you receive the funds. The interest paid on equity loans can possibly be deducted on the borrower's federal tax return.

Whether this is a good option for your family is too complicated a question to be discussed here. Since every individual's income tax situation is unique, you should consult your personal tax preparation firm or a loan consultant for more detailed information regarding the risks and benefits of taking out a home equity loan for the purposes of paying college education expenses.

Be conservative about borrowing money. Do not use loans as a substitute for scholarships, grants, student employment, or lower-interest federal loans simply because you do not want to bother with the FAFSA application or other tedious paperwork. Borrow only as much as you truly *need* for each academic year.

Whose Responsibility Is It?

Before you apply for one of these loans, it is very important that your family has already determined exactly who (student, mother, father, or another relative) will do the borrowing and who exactly will do the paying back.

Repayment responsibility depends on your family's private beliefs. Some families believe that it is the parents who should fulfill their obligation to pay as much as possible toward their children's higher educations. If you share this opinion, your ability to carry the financial burden may mean you have to take out one or more parent loans. Of course, not all people agree with this particular point of view. Plenty of families consider it the student's responsibility to borrow college money, if any loans are needed at all.

QUESTION?

When do I need to begin making repayment on an educational loan?

If you are a student borrower, you are usually given a grace period of somewhere between six and nine months after you have graduated or have ceased to be enrolled as at least a half-time student. If you are a parent borrower, payments are usually expected to begin shortly after your loan has been fully disbursed.

Of course, there is no rule that says the responsibility of paying for college should fall solely upon any one individual's shoulders. Many families have begun to combine the financial responsibility of paying for a college education, with the parents taking out a set portion of their student's educational costs each year in parent loan money. At the same time, the student also borrows a portion of the needed funds to ease the financial burden on the parents.

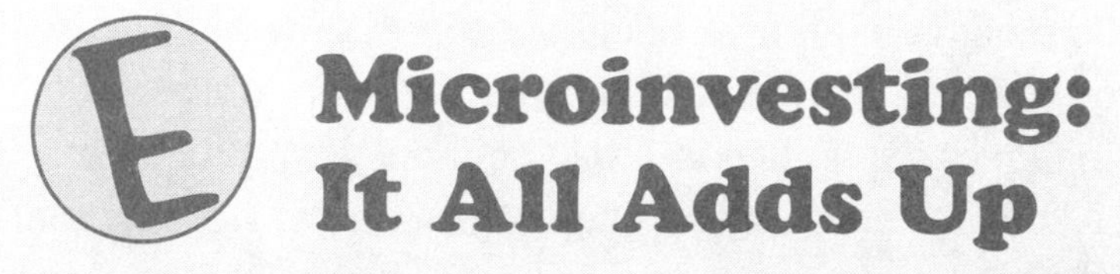

Chapter 12

Microinvesting: It All Adds Up

A penny saved is a penny earned, right? A lot of people seem to think so. In recent years, microinvesting has become the newest savings trend. With credit card use eclipsing cash and even checks, credit card companies are even taking advantage by offering microinvesting opportunities to their customers. A penny may not sound like much of a savings, but every time you save a hundred, you've got another dollar.

Understanding Microinvesting

As everyone knows these days, technology continues to speed forward and the field of electronic financial transactions has advanced by leaps and bounds. Over the last several years, an investment option called microinvesting has emerged. Do you participate in a payroll deduction plan, with funds accruing little by little in an investment account? Do you use a credit card that gives you a rebate at the end of the year for every dollar you charged? Microinvesting means spending or investing money with the aim of getting some back, a little at a time, and earning interest on the growing total. Some people have begun to refer to this minimal style of saving as "microinvesting." Members of these programs can either receive cash benefits periodically or arrange to have them automatically deposited into a Section 529 plan.

Saving little by little over a span of years is a great way to build up some cash reserves, and what better way to save than when you do it by spending? Often, microinvesting is done by collecting a certain amount in a special account every time you make an electronic transaction with a certain card or company.

Is Microinvesting a New Idea?

The microinvesting idea is not really a new one—automatic payroll deduction and dividend reinvestment plans have been around for years. However, as big-name credit card companies have begun to catch on to, not to mention the businesses that accept them, the idea has expanded in a very new way. The credit companies offer cash back on qualified purchases, and this makes the idea of saving small amounts of money at a time even more appealing to the average consumer, who often only has small amounts of extra funds. The really great thing is that investors do not have to change their spending habits. Just registering in a program entitles the member to receive the rebates.

By rolling your microinvesting savings into a Section 529 plan, you can combine some of the really good benefits of a great educational savings plan with a convenient new form of saving.

It's Right for Everybody!

Microinvesting is a great option for people who recognize the need to save for their student's education but who can't contribute the minimum $1,500 required to open up an account in some traditional types of investments. You can contribute any amount, with no minimum investment. It is also a really good option for any frugal-minded person who recognizes that pennies add up to nickels, which add up to dimes, which of course add up to dollars.

Is It Too Late for You?

Like any other investment that you make over time, the earlier you start, the better. That is especially true in the case of microinvesting because the contributions are made in very small amounts. For most people, the best time to start a microinvesting program is when the child is in elementary school. This gives you years to accumulate small amounts before the student enters college. An even better situation would be to start the plan when the child is born. Then you maximize the time and compounding effects of your investment. However, it is never too late to start microinvesting. Some plans allow for the accumulated earnings to go toward repayment of a student loan, so even with a child already in college, microinvesting can be a good idea.

It's Proven to Work

According to a recent report from the Financial Research Corporation, today's microinvesting programs have the earning potential to capture more than $21.7 billion annually in eligible shopping transactions. That means that microinvestors across the country have the potential to accumulate a total of $1.1 billion in collective assets. Shoppers are already spending their money in everyday places like the grocery store, gas station, and restaurants. Theoretically, in the time it took your baby to reach college age, it would be possible to use the principles of microinvesting to build up assets of more than $1 million. No matter how much tuition continues to rise, that should be enough to cover several semesters at even the most expensive schools.

Start Microinvesting

To get started on your microinvesting journey, you simply need to register with a free microinvesting program. Members get rebates on purchases at a wide variety of retailers. Examples of companies that participate in microinvesting programs are Exxon/Mobile, Pizza Hut, Monro Muffler & Brake, Staples, and CVS (to name a few). You can rack up some big bucks if, as a member, you buy or sell a home through a participating real estate brokerage (such as ERA or Coldwell Banker). Additional benefits can be achieved if the member uses a certain credit card to make the purchases or makes purchases from one of many online merchants.

Planning for college expenses when your child is young can mean excellent long-term benefits. Not only will it help your child afford college, it will teach you and your child the rewards of financial planning.

After You Sign Up

After you register with a free program, you can decide which of the participating products you want to buy and at which of the participating businesses you want to shop. In many cases, you don't need to make any changes in your shopping habits at all. These plans are becoming so popular that products and businesses are continually signing up.

These programs also give you the option of rolling your rebates into a Section 529 plan, and you can contribute additional dollars if you want to. Even if you are on a tight budget, you can squeeze out a few dollars a week or month and watch it grow.

Who Likes These Plans?

These plans are especially popular with parents of young children because they have the benefit of compounding interest over a long time. Grandparents can contribute toward a grandchild's educational savings plan without taking any money away from fixed retirement incomes.

With some programs, like the Upromise Plan (described on page 157), current students can also save up money to pay down their existing loans. The really great thing is that more than one person can contribute to a plan, so parents, grandparents, other relatives, generous friends, and the actual student can all register to have their rebates sweep into the same account. Imagine going to a baby shower where everyone registered to have their microinvestment rebates contribute to the lucky little bundle of joy's college fund—not a bad idea!

BabyMint

BabyMint is one company that helps you to accumulate money for college expenses. You register and then buy things from your usual merchants and on your usual credit cards. This is a great example of microinvesting—investing very small amounts over a long period of time. Not to be taken lightly, the Investment Company Institute estimates that 35 percent of the dollar value of consumers' daily purchases could be made available to these "spend and save" programs.

It works quite simply—you sign up free of charge and shop online or in retail stores by using a special BabyMint credit card. As you spend with this card at the affiliated merchants, BabyMint rebates a portion of the purchase price up to a maximum 20 percent, depending upon the merchant.

Does BabyMint Offer Section 529 Options?

BabyMint allows you to invest in any Section 529 plan or to receive your rebate checks directly, to invest as you see fit. BabyMint's proprietary "savings engine" enables individual investors to save toward a child's college tuition without incurring out-of-pocket expenses. Conservative estimates show that by depositing rebates on everyday purchases into an educational savings account, consumers can save as much as $50,000 toward their child's education through BabyMint, depending upon when they enroll.

How Does BabyMint Work?

Parents, family, and friends register with BabyMint at no cost and then receive up to a 20-percent rebate on everyday purchases made through the company's network of 700 retailers. Rebates are also earned when participants redeem BabyMint coupons at more than 127,000 grocery stores and mass merchandisers nationwide. Check the BabyMint Web site (*www.babymint.com*) for a current list of participating merchants.

FACT

Free microinvesting programs enable you to get cash back by using your credit cards for certain purchases, using "loyalty" cards, or by shopping online with special programs. Most programs provide a Section 529 plan for automatic deposit of these funds, and they contribute additional funds as well.

Members get savings opportunities from the following sources, among others:

- Online and off-line shopping
- Gift certificate purchases
- Long-distance providers
- Credit card purchases

Through each of these transaction methods, BabyMint automatically tracks retailer and product rebates and deposits them into the consumer's tax-free Section 529 account or Coverdell education savings account. While there are other microinvesting programs out there, BabyMint is a great option that allows you to invest your savings in whatever investment plan you wish.

Vesdia

The Vesdia Corporation stands at the forefront of the microinvesting revolution. Based in Atlanta, Georgia, this corporation is a leader in coming up with cutting-edge concepts for financial and consumer loyalty solutions. In addition to being the so-called "savings engine" behind their own programs, the company also owns the patent-protected technology used for microinvesting. This technology is licensed by an army of financial institutions, large retailers, and credit card companies, all of whom rely on Vesdia to provide good service to their customers.

What Vesdia Offers the Consumer

Vesdia hosts more than a dozen programs across the United States, as well as some in Canada, serving millions of people with their savings programs daily. Program members may shop at hundreds of leading retailers and/or service providers, receiving a set percentage for each purchase they make. That percentage can then be transferred into a college savings plan or retirement account. The member might even have funds donated to a favorite charity. Vesdia-affiliated loyalty programs help nonprofit organizations, investors, and families save money toward their fund-raising efforts or personal financial goals.

What Vesdia Can Offer You

Vesdia offers innovative savings programs that allow consumers to earn as much as a 30-percent rebate on purchases made through the Vesdia-partnered network—a linked web of more than 500 well-known, widely used retailers (such as Wal-Mart, The Gap, Eddie Bauer, and many others). Retailer transactions, consumer purchases, and product rebates are electronically logged and tracked before being deposited into the member's investment account, or they can be forwarded as donations to a member's favorite charity or nonprofit organization.

Stockback Microinvesting

Stockback is an offspring of the Vesdia Corporation. Stockback hosts a national network of merchants and vendors, and by using Vesdia's "savings engine," the company can help the individual investor on a path of savings toward college, retirement, or any other major event.

Stockback Rebates

Stockback members receive a rebate on purchases made at the stores of participating merchants within the Stockback network (including Blockbuster Video, Dell Computers, and 1-800-Flowers, among others). The transactions are tracked, and rebates are deposited into the investor's account. The programs are designed to address a variety of life expenses and to benefit merchants in the form of consumer loyalty solutions.

Microinvesting is one of the easiest and most convenient ways of saving for college. If you start a microinvesting program in which you contribute a little bit of money each week, or even each month, be sure to stick with it. Regular contributions will give your investment a boost while they sharpen your budgeting and money management skills.

Stockback Loyalty Rewards

Vesdia is now offering brand-new, competitive Stockback Loyalty Rewards credit cards. With these new cards, members can take advantage of rebates on every purchase that they make. This does not just apply to participating merchants. No matter where the member shops or what they buy, rebates are still accrued. This is not a bad deal, considering there are also no annual fees. The best thing about it is that when a member uses one of these Stockback credit cards at a participating in-store merchants, they receive an additional rebate of as much as 7 percent on those purchases.

Stockback Bucks Is Not a Coffee Shop!

A Stockback member's earnings are first collected and stored in the form of Stockback Bucks until a minimum of twenty-five Stockback Bucks have been saved up in a Stockback microinvesting account. As the month in which a member's balance reaches the minimum twenty-five bucks comes to a close, Stockback converts these "Bucks" into actual U.S. dollars (yes, as in legal tender, American currency) at an even value rate (that means one Stockback Buck equals $1 in American money). Once converted, the money is deposited into the member's investment account. If members opt to receive their rebates "in hand," rewards take the form of a monthly check—once that balance has reached the minimum twenty-five Stockback Bucks, of course.

Upromise

Upromise was founded by Michael Bronner, Founder of Digitas, a marketing services firm and a leader in the industry. Bronner is passionately committed to making college education more affordable for families. This passion likely comes from his hard experience as a student who had to rely on scholarships.

During his sophomore year, Bronner paid for a good-sized chunk of his college tuition by starting his own business. This first business used coupons to provide consumer-loyalty services for campus and local merchants. That company, now called Digitas, currently employs more than 1,100 professionals, with *Fortune* 50 client affiliations such as American Express, AT&T, and General Motors.

What do McDonalds, Coca-Cola, Sears, Exxon, L. L. Bean, Giant Eagle, Coldwell Banker, and Dell Computers all have in common? They are all participants in the Upromise microinvesting program, which gives rebates for the money that you spend on purchases and certain services.

How Upromise Works

Upromise was established to give families a better, easier way to save money for college on a regular basis. Upromise encourages families to get a head start by choosing to invest their own money into a college education, and doing so regularly. Upromise's relationships with top investment companies, including The Vanguard Group, make it easy to get started and adopt a long-term savings strategy with tax advantages.

Upromise offers money for college from America's leading companies, such as Citi, McDonald's, and hundreds of others. Members save for college every time they make a purchase from any of thousands of participating grocery, health, and household items. Participating manufacturers include Kellogg's, Coca-Cola, Huggies diapers, Tide, Tylenol, GLAD, and a variety of others. These college savings are available to consumers at over 19,000 grocery stores and drug stores nationwide.

Upromise Investments

Upromise Investments, Inc., is a registered broker-dealer that is completely owned by Upromise. This Upromise subsidiary provides services that make it easier to learn about college savings options by providing members with access to two of America's highest-rated Section 529 plans (one of which is the Upromise College Fund).

Begun in 2002, the Upromise College Fund is a nationally available Section 529 plan sponsored by the State of Nevada. Members of the program can open their accounts and get statements online, as well as choose from several options for Vanguard investments. When members attach their Upromise account to a 529 plan, their Upromise savings are automatically transferred into the plan on a regular basis. Upromise members are also able to invite friends and family to join, which will help to speed up their college savings.

One of the big advantages to microinvesting over a long period of time is the compounding of interest. If you invest $75 per month at 6-percent interest, after twelve years your original $10,800 will be worth $15,761.26. Imagine how much more you could accumulate if you were to invest even more than that per month, or if you earned a higher interest rate or had a few more years to save!

Why Microinvesting Is a Great Idea

Remember, the government considers it the primary responsibility of the family to pay for the student's education, rather than the government, educational institution, or any other organization. You may qualify for some grants, scholarships, and other types of financial aid, but chances are you are still going to have to come up with some contribution as a family. This is a good way to accumulate something toward college expenses without drastically changing the family's lifestyle or feeling like you have made the whole family sacrifice for one student's educational costs.

This type of savings plan is totally automatic, so there is very little that you have to do in order to manage it once you have signed up. Many people in America are not exactly "big savers," mainly because they do not understand all that crazy investment jargon. With microinvesting, you do not have to know anything more than how to register your information. It is innovative, and it is very easy—that means no worry, no muss, no fuss. Just sign up and let it add it up!

The microinvesting program is so easy that anyone, no matter what their level of financial expertise, can start saving money with it. And once you have had even a little success in starting your own little nest egg through rebates, you can start making monthly contributions. You might even develop a habit that will broaden your outlook on financial planning to the point where you begin taking advantage of other types of savings plans in order to meet other major expenses or future goals and plans.

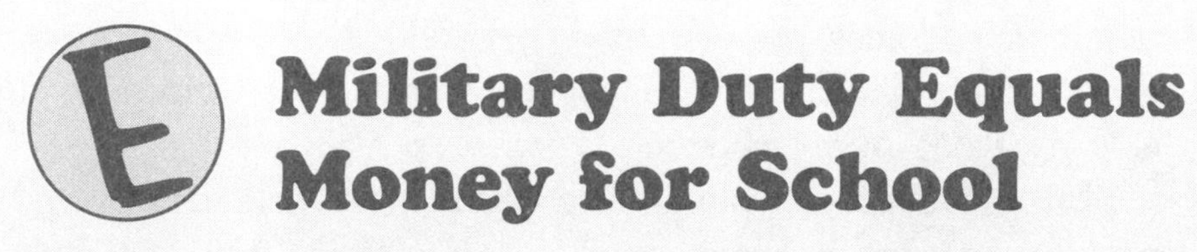

Chapter 13

Military Duty Equals Money for School

Well, you're in trouble now, mister. None of your money has been saved. A Section 529 Plan is wishful thinking at this point. You don't have the grades to get a good scholarship or enough demonstrated financial need to be awarded aid. All I can say is, "Welcome to America, my friend!" Luckily, we live in a country where with a few years of military service, you can completely pay for your education (with enough left over each semester to help pay living expenses).

The Montgomery GI Bill

The Montgomery GI Bill is offered to all enlisted military personnel from the moment they head for boot camp or basic training. Surprisingly, the U.S. government does not try to hide the fact that this money is available. In fact, signing up for the GI Bill is actively encouraged. Even if, as a member of our armed forces, you were to opt out during boot camp processing and choose not to sign up, eventually one of your superior officers would probably insist that you get with the program.

This is not because your participation benefits them in any way. They're just seen what happens to those who separate from the military without the GI Bill. With no way to pay for school, a lot of former military members who opted out of the GI Bill are left with no other option but to work in low or minimum wage jobs, with little hope of ever improving their vocation. (And many of them end up right back in the military in only a few short years—when it was never in their plans to become a career soldier).

If you are male and were born on or after January 1, 1960, and are not currently serving active duty in the U.S. armed forces, you must register with the Selective Service in order to receive federal financial aid.

How the GI Bill Works

First of all, the GI Bill is not exactly free money. You do have to pay for it. In fact, you pay your portion up front within the first year of your enlistment. Your individual portion of payment as soldier, marine, or sailor is $1,200. This amount is paid off with a $50 deduction from every one of your paychecks in your first twelve months of active duty service. That's $100 a month that will be taken out of your pay for at least a full year. For some, that seems like too big a sacrifice. However, when you stop to think of exactly what you end up getting in return for that $1,200, it seems a little crazy not to take the deal.

What the GI Bill Is Worth

On average, the GI Bill is worth about $20,000 for college. You get this benefit in exchange for a four-year stint in whatever branch of service you choose and that $1,200 investment. Think about that. If you join the military but choose not to take advantage of the GI Bill, it would be similar to turning down a legitimate, federally endorsed deal for a payoff of $20,000 in exchange for a $1,200 investment (spread out in twenty-four easy biweekly payments over the span of a year). How smart is it to say no to a deal that can only benefit you?

Can You Put More in and Get More Back?

Yes, you can! If you are already eligible for benefits under the GI Bill (meaning you served in the active duty with an honorable discharge) and you first began your active duty service after June 30, 1985, you can pay an additional $600 toward your education under the GI Bill. Your benefits are upgraded when you use your benefits, on a proportional scale. This means if you had $20,000 for college before, you would now have around $30,000 in exchange for the additional funds.

Enroll Now, Study Later

Although all of the armed services offer the GI Bill, the army has gotten especially enthusiastic about their educational benefits over the last ten years—it's true, the lure of big bucks for tuition is one heck of a recruitment hook for soon-to-be high school graduates. It was in the spirit of such enthusiasm that the army gave birth to the Concurrent Admissions Program, or ConAP. ConAP is a joint agreement between the army and over 1,700 community colleges, vocational schools, and four-year universities across the country. The ConAP program allows people to enlist in the army while stating their intentions to enroll in college during and/or after their term of enlistment. This statement of intent is made at the same time they sign up for duty. This stated intention to enroll is then deferred for up to two years after a soldier is given honorable discharge.

The U.S. Army and participating colleges maintain contact with ConAP soldiers in order to encourage off-duty study and to help these soldiers become familiar with how the ConAP program works.

FACT

A group of participating colleges offers army soldiers the opportunity to complete a college degree and/or vocational certificate online at any given time, as long as they're stationed at a military installation that hosts this program.

The Enigma Called MGIB

As a discharged GI Bill carrier, before you can receive a monthly check, you must already be enrolled in and attending college courses. The difficulty here is that if you do not find some way to pay for your classes before they start, the school will void your enrollment in a heartbeat (or so the policies often state), making the GI Bill benefits void in the process. Although it may seem confusing, the truth is, the program *is* set up to serve you. It just takes a little investigational effort to figure out how to work the system, or at least how to make that system work for you.

Working the System

Most schools offer some form of short-term or emergency loans, which postpone the payment of tuition by shifting numbers around and paying the tuition for you—based, of course, on the understanding that you will pay that money back in full, including interest and fees. (See Chapter 3 for more on emergency loans.) This will cover you until your GI Bill check comes through, and you can use that money to pay back the loan you took from your school.

When completing the FAFSA, you must list the value of your veteran's educational benefits and the number of months during the academic year (July 1 through June 30) in which you will receive them. This information is not used in calculating your expected family contribution. However, federal regulations require that these benefits be counted as part of your financial aid package.

On the first day of the month after you have started attending classes, you will need to verify your enrollment either online (at *www.va.gov*) or over the phone. Many people find that the phone verification is much easier than the online process. You can confirm your enrollment status or handle other matters related to your benefits by calling the Veteran's Affairs Office at (877) 823-2378. In terms of actual minutes, the phone verification is usually faster (and the call is toll free). Listen carefully to the automated menu, and enter your information exactly as it is requested.

Once your call is complete, your enrollment is verified for the month (and the recording tells you what month you are verified for). You should receive your check in seven to ten days (as the recording also makes clear). If you have arranged to receive your GI Bill by direct deposit (with the funds electronically deposited directly into your bank account), the funds will probably be deposited in about seven days. Direct deposit is the fastest way to get your funds and means you don't have to wait those extra three days for a check (which often comes at the last minute).

In December of 2003, as part of the HEROES Act, the U.S. Department of Education changed some of the requirements for federal student aid programs that active-duty military personnel must meet. An example of such a modification is the extension of a student's allowed grace period before he or she starts making repayment of student loans. Under the HEROES Act, rather than the standard six to nine months, the grace period can be up to three years. Individuals should work with their lender to determine the grace period for their specific situation.

What You Get Equals What You Did

Just because you have the GI Bill does not mean that your benefits will be equal to another veteran's benefits. This is because the benefits are based on your time in service and what kind of service that was. Were you on active duty or were you a reservist? Were you in for two years or for four? Did you opt to pay out more money for the GI Bill while in service? All of these factors have an effect on how much you get. However, the bottom line is that you will get money for college—guaranteed.

Veterans who were on active duty receive more money and enjoy more benefits than reservists usually do. Why? It is a matter of investment returns as far as the government and its tax-paying citizens are concerned. We spend the same amount of money on the initial training of an active-duty soldier as on a reservist. However, we receive more work in return from the active-duty service member. The greater return provided on our investment earns that service member access to an increased range of benefits.

The benefits for active duty terms of service are broken down like this:

- Two-year enlistment—Total benefit of $30,000 for college (paid out at approximately $835 per month for 36 academic months)
- Three-year enlistment—Total benefit of $37,000 for college (paid out at approximately $1025 per month for 36 academic months)
- Four-year enlistment—Total benefit of more than $42,000 (paid out at approximately $1,165 per month for 36 academic months)
- Five-year enlistment—Total benefit of $47,000 (paid out at approximately $1,300 per month for 36 academic months)
- Six-year enlistment—Total benefit of $50,000 (paid out at approximately $1,400 per month for 36 academic months)

Once your full enlistment has been served, you can leave the military and draw your GI Bill benefits to go back to school.

What You Get for Reserve Duty

As mentioned before, reservists do not earn as much back as a soldier who has served on active duty, though they do receive college benefits. For example, army reservists can earn more than $10,000 for college in a snap. However, there is just one catch—they have to enlist for no less than a term of six years.

Be sure to inform your institution's financial aid office if your status with the military changes, especially if you have been called up to active duty. It is essential for the financial aid office to be made aware of your situation so that administrators can take the necessary steps to preserve your financial aid status so you still have your benefits when you return.

Maybe the disparity in benefits seems unfair. The army reserve makes a good-hearted attempt to make that up to you. They will even help you earn more money for college. However, once again there is a catch—you have to be assigned to critical skill positions or critical units. Such assignments can increase the benefits for a reservist to over $22,000.

The army reserve calls such a program a GI Bill "kicker." Depending on your occupational specialty and what unit you are assigned to during a critical assignment, your "kicker" could mean an extra $100 to $350 a month for full-time attendance. This may not sound like much to you now, but when you're in school and the bills start piling up, that extra money each month will be more than welcome.

Your Education Benefits

You are not restricted to a traditional four-year university in order to get an education using the GI Bill. The GI Bill is intended to help veterans find a vocational skill that will allow them to enter the civilian workforce productively, and not all occupations require a four-year degree. Just about any kind of training or educational course you take for the purpose of finding or improving your vocational skills can be eligible for GI Bill endorsement. Degree and technical certificate programs are just one example. Other possibilities include flight training, apprenticeships, on-the-job-training, and certain kinds of correspondence courses.

Members of the military should keep a hard copy file of their leave and earnings statements (LES), even after receiving their honorable discharge/separation papers. These records may help you to answer questions on the FASFA should you need to file for financial aid immediately after your discharge.

National Guard

The "selected reserve" category includes reserves for all branches of the U.S. Armed Forces: army, navy, air force, marine corps, and coast guard, as well as the army national guard and the air national guard. What does this mean? It means there's not a lick of difference between the GI Bill benefits offered to reservists and national guardsman. Money shouldn't be a factor if you happen to find yourself torn between these two options.

The GI Bill still provides national guardsmen with as much as thirty-six months of tuition benefits for the purposes of college, vocational courses, business classes, and certain correspondence courses. However, national guardsmen (unlike reservists) are restricted by tighter rules concerning what courses they're allowed to take. Some courses of study that are available to reservists are not endorsed for national guardsmen.

Other Benefits of Military Service

Feeling gung-ho yet? Well, the fun is just beginning, because your military training, courses, and occupational specialty can all count for college credit. A survey conducted by the American Council on Education found that the average number of academic credits awarded from military transcripts for 1998 was fourteen semester hours. This saves you tuition dollars and classroom time!

Receiving College Credit

Policies vary from one college to another, and they can also change depending on the program of study you have chosen. When you contact a school, have your paperwork on hand. If you are a discharged vet, you will need to dig up your DD-214 forms (those are the papers they handed you and said not to lose when you were discharged). If you no longer know where to find your DD-214, you will need to complete a form called an SF 180 in order to verify your military transcript.

Not all military training courses appear on a military transcript, so keep track of the records for all the classes you have taken for military training. Look over your military transcript to be sure it is still accurate. In certain extreme cases, as many as five or more years of military experience can qualify for several full-time semesters' worth of college credit.

FACT

All veterans should consult their local veteran's administration office—almost all college campuses have one—to find out about their specific benefits. Selected reservists should also be aware of the fact that their entitlements under the GI Bill will permanently expire fourteen years from the date that they became eligible for the program or from the date that they left their branch of the selected reserve.

When requesting a transcript to be sent to your school, it should be sent directly from the transcript office to the school (not to you and then the school). However, you should also request an unofficial transcript for your review. Request this personal copy before you request the transcript that's going to be sent to the school administrators. That way, you can have any necessary corrections made. Remember that each branch of service has its own unique transcript request forms and process. Know which you are using, and be sure it is correct.

A Foot in the Door

Joining the military can be a lot like joining an exclusive club. For members of the marine corps this rings is especially true. They are more fanatical about brotherhood than a college fraternity. Such camaraderie can be a great advantage when you finally get your walking papers and enter the civilian world. Many human resource administrators are on the lookout for military veterans with good records and honorable discharges. (You may find that many administrators have served time in the military themselves.) That piece of information on your resume alone is sometimes enough to get you an interview when you might otherwise not have gotten so much as a form letter.

JROTC and Other High School Military Programs

Junior ROTC leadership education develops good citizenship, self-confidence, and self-discipline. Leadership classes introduce cadets to training elements such as leadership, military customs, drill and ceremonies, uniform inspections, physical fitness training, marksmanship, and Marine Corps history. Cadets are required to participate in civic service, wear a uniform, and dress up in nice civilian clothes at least twice a month. Joining JROTC while in high school can help you become eligible for a number of scholarships.

To get a jump-start on a military career, and improve your odds of getting accepted into an ROTC program, you may want to join a military program while you're still in high school. Programs like JROTC, the Naval Sea Cadet Corps, and the Civil Air Patrol are all open to high school students. They will give anyone looking at a future in the military a nice jump on the competition.

ROTC

The Reserve Officer's Training Corps, or ROTC, is a program for college students who intend to become officers in the military after graduating. (This is not the same as JROTC, which is for high school students.) This is not an umbrella program, and the requirements for eligibility may change from one branch of the service to another. Anyone who is interested in ROTC participation should be sure that they know what they are getting themselves into before signing anything. For example, the marine corps requires that every marine go to boot camp, while other branches of service count office training as a boot camp equivalent. Some ROTC programs count your military science education while in college as "basic training."

JROTC Order of Daedalian Scholarships

The Order of Daedalians honors all World War I aviators who were commissioned as officers and as military pilots before the 1918 armistice. These pilots were the first to fly airplanes in wartime. The organization funds a comprehensive awards program, supports the military services, and donates funds to other aerospace and flight-related activities. It is intended to foster patriotism while encouraging good character and integrity in young Americans. The Daedalian Foundation's scholarship program also promotes JROTC students with a focus of study in aerospace disciplines.

FACT

Some examples of military scholarship programs are the Reserve Officer Training Corps (ROTC), Air Force Reserve Officer Training Corps (AFROTC), and Naval Reserve Officers Training Corps (NROTC, for both the navy and marine corps).

Daedalian JROTC Awards Offered

There is a veritable gold mine of scholarship awards available to high school students participating in the JROTC program. No matter what branch of JROTC you participate in, there is a scholarship that you are eligible for. Let's take a look at a number of these JROTC exclusive scholarships:

- The Daedalian JROTC Achievement Award is presented each year to outstanding third-year cadets who are attending one of the participating high schools.
- Begun in 1978, the Daedalian Matching Scholarship Program is an annual cash award, given to match flight scholarships that are given to worthy students with a strong desire to become military pilots.
- The Major General Lucas V. Beau Flight Scholarship is another award from the Daedalian Order. It is announced each year to civil air patrol cadets who demonstrate a desire for military careers in aviation and who use the civil air patrol for ground and flight training leading to a private pilot's license.
- Daedalian Air Force ROTC Scholarships are awarded yearly to air force ROTC cadets who have performed in an outstanding manner.
- The Daedalian Army ROTC Scholarships are awarded annually to the previous year's outstanding nonscholarship MS-IV Aviation Branch ROTC cadets.
- The Daedalian Naval ROTC Scholarships are presented yearly to senior naval ROTC cadets who possess the desire and capability to become future naval aviators.
- The Daedalian Foundation Descendants Scholarship Program offers a number of cash scholarships for the study of aerospace engineering and flight and is awarded annually to descendants of members of the Daedalian Order.
- The Daedalian Colonel Charles Getchell Memorial Scholarships consist of five awards presented each year to outstanding ROTC cadets. This program was made possible by a donation from Mrs. Getchell, widow of founder Colonel Charles Getchell.

Military scholarships are awarded on the basis of physical, humanitarian, or academic merit, and not on financial need. After graduating from college, recipients are usually required to serve in a branch of the U.S. Armed Forces for a set number of years.

How JROTC Benefits You

If you have at least two years of active membership in any JROTC-related, paramilitary program, it can mean good things for you when and if you decide that the military route is for you. If you have two years of membership, you may enter military service with an automatic promotion to E-2, one step up in the enlisted ranks from E-1, where everyone else is at the beginning (not a big jump up the chain, but it's at least a start). Your years of JROTC participation must not be consecutive, and they must also be in the same branch of JROTC.

Chapter 14

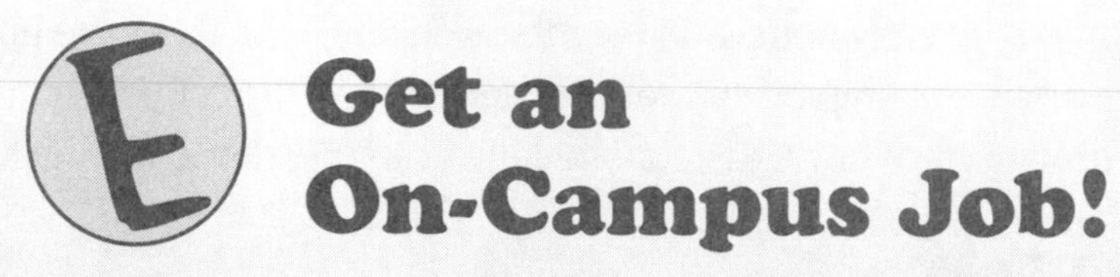

Get an On-Campus Job!

It would be ideal to get scholarships and grants to pay for your education, and it would also be a good idea to have money already saved up or invested for your educational future. But reality is sometimes different. If you find yourself without money, there is one surefire way to get some—you have to get a job! That's right. Plenty of students are getting their college educations the old-fashioned way, by working their way through school. If they can do it, so can you.

Why Work on Campus?

Take a look around your college campus. You will probably see buildings everywhere. The important thing is that most of these buildings employ students. The campus library as well as the dining halls, student center, campus gym, and recreation center are often dependent upon student workers to keep the buildings open in the evening hours and over the weekends. As far as the university is concerned, student employees are a big necessity in order for the campus to continue running smoothly and economically from one day to the next.

Work Is Good for You

As a student, you'll reap personal benefits from working on campus as well as a monetary payoff. Statistics indicate that college students who work (in on- or off-campus jobs) do better in their college careers and often have higher GPAs than those who do not work at all. Other benefits of on-campus student employment include the opportunity to build business/academic contacts for the future, improved confidence, and improved time management and organization skills.

Before being hired to a particular position, students should consider any commitments they have before taking that job. No more than ten hours a week should be scheduled for work until the student gets a sense of what their class and extracurricular commitments are going to be like for the semester.

Aren't All On-Campus Jobs Boring and Minimum Wage?

There are a number of reasons why an on-campus job is better for students. For starters, you won't pay as much for transportation, and it won't take you a lot time to get to and from work. Jobs range from clerical and customer service positions, such as a wide variety of library positions, to jobs with professors around the campus. Students are encouraged to seek jobs in their interest areas, giving them an opportunity to gain experience within a field. The best way to find work is by contacting faculty within the department of interest. If you are interested in physics, you should contact the physics faculty and see about finding a research job. Any college's career services center can help students locate work on campus.

Even though many of the jobs are minimum wage, the upside to having an on-campus job is more than enough to make you forget about the downside. Even if your starting pay is low, by coming back to the same job year after year you are likely to earn a raise. (It would probably be a big plus if you didn't have to look for a job again next year, too.)

The biggest of the upsides is that you are better equipped to handle scheduling work around your classes. Off-campus jobs often require shifts of more than six hours in a row, whereas on-campus jobs can be scheduled for as little as those two hours between your morning classes.

Undoubtedly, the best part is that you'll never get stuck working on a holiday! On-campus student employees do not have to work on holidays when the university is closed! And working during exam week? No problem. On-campus student employees also get to have days off during the days of exam week. Your boss at an off-campus job likely isn't going to care much about your exams; all he wants is for you to show up at work as usual.

If you plan to work on campus when you become a college student, find out what the requirements are for working and how you can get a job. Some colleges and universities assign jobs to students, while others allow the students to apply for them. It's very important for you to know in advance what you must do to find employment so that you aren't left without any options.

Federal Work Study

Think of a job in a federal work-study program as a self-help way of getting financial aid. Why self-help? Because it's up to you! This means that you have to do some work in order to receive the aid. Loans are also considered self-help because you have to get a job later in order to pay the money back.

In the case of federal work study, students must work in order to receive a paycheck. Federal work study is a campus-based program, which means that individual schools receive a certain amount of government funds and are then able to decide how they wish to distribute those taxpayer dollars. Institutions of higher education are also required to contribute a certain percentage of their own funds to the working student's wages.

Work Study Job Options

Jobs that are made available through the federal work-study program must be used to benefit students who have a demonstrated financial need. A wide variety of jobs is usually available, from office worker to research assistant to computer tutor, for example. Ideally, the job should be relevant to the student's academic area of study.

These jobs, while commonly located on the college campus, also have the potential to end up being off campus. Typically, if the work-study job is performed off campus, then it will probably be at a local nonprofit agency. Schools are required to pay out at least minimum wage to work-study students, and they must do so at least once per month in this program.

FACT

Consider a community service job. Unless it receives a waiver, every institution that participates in the federal work-study program must use at least 7 percent of its federal allocation every year to pay the federal share of wages to students employed in community service jobs. These jobs may be on campus or at any local nonprofit organization.

Getting Paid

Jobs for undergraduate students are required to pay hourly wages. You will be awarded a certain dollar amount of federal work-study money as part of your financial aid package, and you cannot exceed that maximum earnings amount for the academic year.

Undergraduate work-study students often receive their money in the form of a paycheck, the amount of which depends on how many on-the-clock hours they actually worked. Direct deposit to either a checking or savings account is also possible upon request. Graduate students may be paid hourly as well, but they also have the option of getting a salary through this program.

Pay close attention to how much you have earned throughout the academic year. You may have to stop working when you have reached your limit if your institution cannot or will not increase your maximum earnings ceiling.

Institutional Employment

Most colleges and universities allocate funds for students who either want or need to work but for some reason are not qualified for participation in the federal-work study program. Colleges call their institutional work programs by a number of different names—campus employment, college work, institutional jobs, and so on. Just because a program like that is in place does not mean that the institution will necessarily give any student who wants work a job. This is especially true if you do not qualify for a particular work-study program. Usually, due to budget constraints and policy, institutions fund only a limited number of their own work-study positions.

Institutional employment tends to be very similar to working in federal work-study positions, and jobs are usually found and performed on campus. If you don't qualify to participate in a federal work-study program but you still want to work, you should ask about the possibility of institutional employment, and the sooner the better. It is better to have that option officially on your financial aid package and decide not to work than to wait until you find a campus job and then find out you are too late to get a campus employment award.

If possible, try to find an on-campus job that complements your academic interests. Working in a job related to your academic strengths will be more interesting, and it might also be a good experience for any future employment.

Grant-Funded Positions

Grant-funded job positions are usually not advertised. Roughly speaking, here is what happens when these positions are being filled. A professor applies for a grant through either a government agency or some philanthropic organization in order to do some kind of research project during the summer. If the grant is approved, the professor will need students to help with the project. Professors usually ask students they already know. However, they sometimes consider another promising student who would be willing to work on the research project until someone else is found to perform the job.

Tracking Down Grant Jobs

Do not just assume that these jobs are there for the taking. Instead of just hoping you happen to be chosen, do a little asking around yourself. Check with an academic advisor to see if any professors are planning on doing research projects and hiring student assistants.

Be Proactive

Ask professors, especially those who instruct classes that you have done well in, if they are looking for research assistants. Perhaps you had a class last semester with a professor who is now the recipient of grant funding. Maybe that professor would not have thought of hiring you, or even asking you, simply because you are not currently in any of her classes. However, if you were to approach her about the grant-funded research work that she is conducting, you will not likely be forgotten when the time comes.

If you plan to work on campus during the summer, ask early about possible summer employment opportunities. There may not be as many jobs available as there are during the academic year. Then again, there may be more. Either way, you know the saying: "The early bird catches the good on-campus summer job."

Be a Resident Advisor

Here is a job that is just perfect for some students! And some colleges offer big financial incentives for students in this position, too. Being a resident advisor (RA) is kind of like being an activities coordinator, babysitter, mediator, and policy enforcement officer all in one. It is a job with a lot of responsibility, but colleges usually provide plenty of training and resources.

Ideally, students who are RAs should be leaders who like to take charge and who get along well with their peers. They should be outgoing and not afraid to deal with dorm problems as they arise—such as noisy residents, roommates who do not get along, stressed-out students, and so on. You might be thinking, "Why in the world would someone want a job like that?" Well, some students like the responsibility and are good at it. It is the perfect job for them.

RA Benefits

The pay and benefits of being a resident advisor can be fantastic. Some institutions actually pay their RAs as much as two to three times more than what they pay students working in other on-campus jobs. It is also common for institutions to completely waive the room and board charges for RAs. Sometimes this even includes the entire cost of meal plans. These two factors alone could represent a substantial amount of money that would be freed up and go exclusively toward paying your tuition!

An RA package has a roughly estimated monetary worth around $5,000 for a single academic year. Don't forget that an RA job would also look excellent on a resume when you're eventually ready to enter the workforce. If you can handle managing kids in a dorm, you can handle just about anything.

Colleges like to hire students just as much as students like to be hired. The biggest reason for hiring a work-study student is often because it is the most economical way to find a temporary and low-cost employee. Through the federal work study program, schools get a certain amount of money from the government, which they use to pay wages to students doing necessary work on campus.

The Downside to RA Work

All dorm residents have a residential advisor hired by the residential life office to interact and provide fun, companionship, supervision, and so on. Part of your job as an RA usually includes hosting, organizing, and presenting a complete series of group events or presentations every single semester. Be aware that colleges are big on seeing students "turn out" in support for their programs. As an RA, you would be expected to make that happen. This can be a source of extra stress if you've already got a full course load and exams and papers to worry about.

There can be some social downsides to being an RA as well, especially if you like to have every single weekend off and to yourself. A big part of being an RA is doing the right thing and being responsible even when you want to do what everyone else is doing. It means breaking up a party down the hall that has gotten out of hand, or asking the partygoers on the floor above you to keep it down—at 3 A.M. on the last morning of finals week, when the only thing you want to do is get some sleep before your last exam.

Become a Tutor

Do not forget one of your biggest assets when trying to find a job—all that brainpower you've accumulated! All colleges provide tutors for students who need a little extra help in difficult courses. If you did well in a class, ask your professor about tutoring possibilities the next semester or next year. Imagine getting paid for sitting in a tutor station and helping students who drop by for assistance occasionally—not a bad part-time job. Maybe you can even get some of your own homework done if it is a slow day.

FACT

Every educational institution needs tutors in just about every subject, from English to mathematics. If you are a strong student in certain subjects, investigate tutoring opportunities. Your academic abilities might land you a job, even if you are not qualified for federal work study or campus employment programs.

Advertise!

If you are really ambitious in the area of tutoring, you can advertise in the local newspaper, at the YMCA, or at other public buildings such as the library or post office. Let local primary and public schools know that you are available to tutor elementary and/or high school students. There are always younger students out there who need a little extra help in math, reading, or science. If you do a good job, word will spread fast. There are an infinite number of parents in this country who are willing to pay whatever it takes to see better grades on their child's report card. That money is yours for the taking if you have what it takes to be a tutor.

A job as a tutor can benefit you in another way besides just generating extra income; it can sharpen your communication skills, as well. When companies hire new employees, they tend to seek out applicants who have the appropriate education and experience as well as the ability to express themselves well. Employers also look for prospects with the ability to convey information and new concepts to clients with both confidence and clarity. Having tutorial experience on your resume may just be the leg up you need.

Tutoring Does Not Mean Helping Others Cheat!

The job of a tutor is to help the student understand and apply particular concepts in difficult courses. This does not translate doing the student's work. The tutor's job is to better the student's odds of success, not help him skate through by giving him the answers; to work toward improving the student's learning methods and comprehension, not giving them the minimum they need to know. Tutors should provide their students with a stress-free environment, increase each student's self-confidence, and be a source of motivation for them. That does not mean bringing them to tears by frustrating or badgering them or making them feel stupid.

Respect your students by maintaining confidentiality. Respect ethics by not being bribed or tempted into helping someone cheat. Keep a log so you are able to provide a record of each tutoring session. This gives you and your students a sense of accomplishment (and provides tangible results for their parents, if necessary). A log also prevents you from being held liable if one of your students is caught cheating and decides to point the finger at you.

Remember that if you do decide to be a tutor, you need to do it because helping others learn is something close to your heart. This is not the kind of job you can do simply for the money. That attitude will not help anyone improve.

Popular Tutor Subjects

Tutors offer students individual attention, a rarity in today's crowded classrooms. Tutors can teach to whatever level each student needs, allowing them to move at their own pace without the stress of a professor looking over their shoulders. Big, nationwide tutoring franchises are now providing services in a number of communities. Some self-employed tutors charge (and actually get) as much as $160 an hour for helping college students with higher level math or science classes. Not bad, right?

While math is (and likely always has been) the subject in which tutors are most popular, there is really no end to the number of subjects in which a tutor is useful. Tutors are used by all kinds of strokes and folks—from computer geniuses struggling with history to older students who are a bit slower than the younger generations in grasping computer skills. Some parents hire a tutor for a learning-disabled child so their student can keep up, worried they will get left behind should they fail to master certain basic skills or struggle to pass some core requirements. It is considered a specialty in tutoring to be able to work with students who have learning disabilities.

The big-money market for tutors these days is tutors who coach students on how to pass a college entrance exam. Standardized admissions tests—such as the ACT, ERB, PSAT, SSAT, SAT, and TOEFL—scare some parents and students absolutely stiff. This anxiety seems so intense that it has begun driving some students to begin preparing for these exams as much as a year in advance. Here's where you come in. Sign them up, and get to work.

Chapter 15

Get an Off-Campus Job!

"When all else fails, you can always flip burgers!" Does this phrase sound familiar? Restaurant jobs are often a good option for college students who are a little short on cash, but if a food-related position is not exactly what you had in mind, don't worry. There are plenty of other options for college students, even with their needs for part-time hours and flexible schedules. So, while fast food is definitely one of the options listed in this chapter, it is not the only one.

May I Take Your Order, Please?

Today's working college student is no longer restricted to the sole option of taking a position behind a fast-food counter. However, there are those who, obviously, prefer working in the fast-paced environment of establishments such as McDonald's, Jack-in-the-Box, or other restaurants of this type. Just as with any kind of part-time job, students working in fast-food positions have to take the good with the bad. In this respect, it does not matter whether you are a drive-through attendant or a stockbroker on Wall Street—there are going to be some things that you enjoy about the job and other things that make you want to consider the benefits of some other kind of job.

When applying for a part-time job, never put "minimum wage" in the section that asks what you expect as a starting salary. This tells the employer that you plan to do no more than required for you to turn a paycheck. Always ask for at least a quarter an hour above minimum wage. The worst that can happen is that they'll offer you $5.15 anyway. How you respond is up to you.

Opportunities at McDonald's

Working at McDonald's offers a lot more opportunity than one might think. There is always room for advancement, both inside the individual restaurant and within the company. The possibilities for advancement as a McDonald's employee seems to go pretty high—to the top of the food chain, one might say. Many of McDonald's middle and senior managers or franchisees began working at a McDonald's restaurant in entry-level positions. Several of the McDonald's corporation's top executives began their careers at the entry level. So, if you want to work your way up in this chain, it looks like starting at the bottom might be the way to go. Besides, the company philosophy seems to focus on the ideals of teamwork, dependability, and responsibility—what you might call the traits of success.

There are over 12,000 McDonald's restaurant managers in this country, and a majority of them began their careers manning deep-fat fryers and wearing groovy drive-through headsets. The average McDonald's manager is responsible for running a million-dollar business—not the worst way to start out your life as a graduate student with an MBA.

Jack-in-the-Box

Jack-in-the-Box is another fast-food restaurant. It is located mainly in the western part of the United States, although they have some locations in the South and Midwest. Like other restaurants of this type, they offer great opportunities for advancement. Job opportunities for students include a position called shift leader, an hourly position that requires you to perform a lead role in overseeing and operating workstations. Other opportunities range from management trainee all the way up to general manager. Base pay for the general manager position ranges from $30,500 to $59,000 per year; bonuses are based on guest service and profit performance, and they average approximately $15,000 per year. You're not going to make it to this level while still in school, of course, but that wouldn't be a terrible job to end up with, would it?

Senator John Kerry has proposed an increase in the federal requirements for minimum wage that would raise it to $7 by the year 2007. This would be a $1.85 increase from the current minimum wage, which has not changed from $5.15 since it was set in 1997. That is the longest gap between minimum wage increases since 1949, during Harry Truman's presidency.

Food Service—Not Always Greasy!

When many college students consider the idea of a part-time job in the food service industry, they automatically think about flipping burgers in the hot, greasy kitchen of a local fast-food joint. While there is definitely nothing wrong with that, you should realize that there are a variety of other jobs available in food service. For example, you might consider working in one of the nicer, more upscale restaurants in your college community.

The money a student can make working at a restaurant can be fantastic (especially compared to minimum wage) once you factor in your tips, and the hours are usually perfect for a working college student, since evenings and weekends are often the busiest times. This means that you would be more than able to work shifts that would not clash with your class schedule. Certain "sit-down" chain restaurants actually prefer to have college students working as their hostesses and servers—for example, Red Lobster, Olive Garden, Outback Steakhouse, and other similar establishments.

Bus Tables

True, cleaning up after other people can be a really nasty job. Most students see this as a kind of lower wage, entry-level position that you have to work in first, in order to get bumped up to one of the better-tipping positions. However, while you're waiting to move up, working on the bus staff of a popular, busy restaurant can be well worth it, especially if you are working at a place where they give the bus staff a cut of the house tips.

Wait Staff

In an upscale diner such as Denny's or International House of Pancakes, there is an opportunity to make some really good money in tips. However, you may have to work some very odd hours in order to reap the best rewards. For example, if you work at an all-night diner that's located near a college campus, one of the best times to work is the shift that runs into the hours just after midnight. The wee hours of the morning are "tip central" at a college diner. Why? Because, in most states, this is about the time when the bars and dance clubs begin to close down for the night. The incoming patrons are going to be tired and probably hungry. Tolerate that with a smile, and you will have no problem. Be their savior for the night by bringing them their caffeine and food, and you will be surprised at just how easily they can separate their cash from their wallets for a nice-sized tip.

Good News for Hospitality Majors

If you're planning to get a college education centered on restaurant management, working in a restaurant now would be the perfect job for you. This is especially true if you find one with a specific program in place to help students like you. For example, Red Lobster has developed close ties with many universities, offering hospitality management programs to students. Red Lobster has a variety of opportunities for students to enhance their education both during college and after they graduate. Red Lobster's college recruitment program also offers internships during your college education as well as full-time management placement when you graduate.

FACT

Being part of a college recruitment program might be just the advantage you need to get your foot in the door with a good organization with plenty of opportunity for the future. Hey, it definitely couldn't work against you!

Through its internship program, Red Lobster attempts to give its interns significant exposure to every area of the restaurant management world. Interns strengthen their management skills, participating in a wide range of professional development exercises. The best part is, you get paid for it! Interns receive ten weeks of on-the-job training during the summer term, just prior to their senior year of college. During the internship, students average about forty hours of work every week and are paid $10 an hour. To be eligible for a Red Lobster college internship, applicants must be both an upcoming senior in college and be majoring in a hospitality field (such as those for restaurants, hotels, or food service management).

Even if this particular program does not sound quite right for you, keep in mind that this is not the only such opportunity out there. The more on-the-job experience you can get in your chosen field now, the better your resume will look when it comes time to graduate and start looking for your full-time career.

Other Jobs That Tip

Sometimes it can be better for working students to have a part-time job that comes with tips than it is for them to have a job with a salary or high hourly wages. Students should remember to never pass on a job just because the hourly wages sound ridiculously low. Keep in mind that minimum wage is the standard, so if an employer offers you a salary below federal minimum wage, the job likely comes with tips to supplement it—either that or the place is into some kind of shady business (in which case, get out of there and don't look back!)

Bartending

You may have heard that the tips are great for bartenders. This is usually true. However, the kind of establishment has a lot to do with the kind of tips a bartender makes in a night. Just because a place is packed, do not assume this means plenty of money in tips. It has more to do with what kind of crowd frequents the establishment. For example, the tavern near campus may have every Tom, Dick, and Jane walk in during happy hour. However, these are broke students scraping together change for penny draft nights—do you really think that they have extra money to spend on a tip?

Check your state's laws about bartending to see whether you are old enough to do this legally. Some states allow students under the age of twenty-one to work behind the bar. Also, find out what type of training is required before you apply. Some bartenders receive training on the job, but there are also short-term bartending schools all across the country that offer certificate programs.

In order to learn where the tips are, frequent a bar for a couple of days, during at least two separate shifts (afternoon, evening, and late night are good times). Try to take notice of how fast the tip jars fill up. Better yet, start up a conversation with the current bartender and throw in something along the lines of, "You guys must make great tips here." Here is a free hint. That question has a much better chance of getting a truthful response if you ask it while you are putting money into the tip jar (make sure the bartender sees you do it). Otherwise, the bartender may think you are a cheapskate who is just trying to make yourself feel better about not leaving a tip. She may tell you that the tips are lousy just to manipulate you into forking up a buck.

If you like to drive and want to make some money doing it, see if your campus has a shuttle service that needs student drivers. You may even want to offer out your own services—post flyers advertising rides to the mall or the airport.

Hotel Work

Many jobs in the hotel industry earn tips from customers, from doorman to valet to the exalted position of concierge. A hotel is always open and ready to serve its guests, which means the hours are variable—the perfect situation for a student with a busy schedule. As in restaurants, you might have to start at the bottom, but with a good attitude and a reliable record, you'll be in the tips in no time.

Non-Tipping Job Options

Just because a job does not come with tips doesn't mean that the pay is lousy. Hourly wages are regular and dependable, unlike tips—you'll always have a good idea of how much you can expect to earn in a week. However, it can also mean that you will work a lot harder and a lot longer for your money. It can also mean battling your coworkers to make sure you get enough hours in each week. If the store you work in hires too many employees, they will often cut a little from everyone's hours before they will fire someone.

Grocery Bagger

This job can be extremely hard on a person physically, especially on that person's feet, and often it is not very rewarding. Being a grocery bagger used to be considered a pretty nice "tipping job" for local high school and college kids. However, the times have changed, and many of the big grocery chains have even started up corporate policies that forbid the tipping of their sackers/baggers. The nice thing about this job is that it keeps you active. Also, you don't have to worry about taking your job responsibilities home with you.

This is one job that leaves your gray matter free to think about more important things—like your studies.

Grocery Stocker

This is often a low-stress job. Usually, a grocery stocker's work is done during the late hours of the night, when there are few or no customers in the store. This job will rarely interfere with your classes, as long as you make sure you are getting sleep at regular, eight-hour intervals. On the flip side of the coin, this is a job that makes burning yourself out very easy if you go to your classes all day long and are stocking groceries into the wee hours of the night.

Convenience Stores

Two words: job security. Not many other kinds of job offer work possibilities in any of a dozen stores in each of a thousand other cities across the country. You can go home for the summer and work at another location without losing any seniority. However, you should keep in mind that convenience stores are also a very popular target for criminal activity and armed robbery. There will always be a certain level of danger as long as you are employed at one, especially if you ever end up working during the graveyard shift. If you choose convenience-store work, make sure you work for a company that puts its employees' safety at the top of the priority list.

Teaching at the Y

The YMCA and YWCA often need instructors for a variety of different classes, especially in athletics—aerobics, martial arts, gymnastics, and so on. Perhaps you have been a lifelong yoga practitioner? Do you know how to teach someone to cross-stitch? Any number of these things might be able to land you a job at the local Y, or any other recreation center. To find out what subjects are most in demand, call up some local branches and inquire.

Internships

Nowadays, the theory is that an education plus job experience prepares a student for the real-world job market. Good jobs after graduation are hard to come by, and those students who have a strong education and experience in their fields certainly have an advantage. One way students are getting the work experience they need is through internships. Some academic programs even require that students in the program complete an internship as part of the graduation requirements.

Are Interns Paid?

Let's say you want to (or, sometimes, you have to) do an internship. Internships can be paid or unpaid, for academic credit or not. As you investigate your internship possibilities, it is possible to find one that pays money, so always look for this option first. Start looking early—if you need a summer internship, start looking during the fall semester. Start by applying only for those internships that pay money.

Finding Internships

Most colleges and universities have an internship or career services office. That's a good place to start investigating internship options. Academic departments and area businesses might also have internship possibilities that aren't advertised through the college internship office. Take the initiative to stop by and find out.

In addition, the U.S. State Department and other federal agencies in the United States offer internships (most of which are unpaid) to undergraduate and graduate students. Applications for these are due each year by November 1 for summer internships, March 1 for fall, and July 1 for winter. State and city governments have many internship possibilities that often get overlooked. Jobs that require working with members of congress or state government are also available through governmental internships.

Some students go directly to selected businesses and ask if they would be willing to create a paid internship opportunity (or convert a summer job into an internship) for them. When the right student makes inquiries to the right company, it can be a match made in heaven—because in such a case everybody wins, both the intern and the company!

When Internships Do Not Pay

If you are required to take an internship that does offer monetary compensation, you may want to inquire at your institution's financial aid office, dean's office, and/or career or internship office to see if there are grants or cash stipends available. You may not be getting paid, but a little money is better than none. With a small stipend you may be able to at least afford to get some of your resulting internship expenses covered.

Which Internship Is Right for You?

There are more internships in this world than we could ever possibly hope to list here. However, just because there are so many of them does not mean that they are easy to get. In fact, there are probably more students trying to get internships than there are internships in existence. Therefore, a competitive attitude is often a key attribute for those hoping to secure an internship—paid or otherwise. The best way to fight an enemy is to first know your enemy, so the following sections provide a few examples of the kinds of high-profile internships available in the modern workforce.

Work for the State Department

A U.S. State Department internship is an impressive way to explore a career in diplomatic relations. Most of them are unpaid; however, free housing is usually provided. To be eligible for these internships, applicants must be U.S. citizens who are undergraduates or graduate students who plan to continue on with their education until they have actually graduated. You can apply for these internships online via the State Department's Web site. For more information on federal student job opportunities, visit the U.S. Government's student job Web site at *www.studentjobs.gov.*

Join the Peace Corps

The U.S. Peace Corps offers quite possibly some of the best and highest-paying entry-level intern jobs for anyone interested in humanitarian work in foreign locations. Unlike the state department jobs mentioned earlier, you will not be rubbing elbows with people in high places. The Peace Corps expects a lot of you. This means getting your hands dirty by living and working with the native peoples of your assigned region. To be eligible, applicants must be U.S. citizens.

Most Peace Corps work is meant for people with a bachelor's degree and requires a two-year commitment. However, there are exceptions with certain intern positions. Despite your position or internship, the Peace Corps pays for all of your expenses plus an additional stipend of as much as over $6,000 for resettlement costs at the end of your service.

Training and support is provided to you, not to mention invaluable experience in the way of the world. Educational loans can often be deferred, and some may even be partially canceled should you decide to join the Peace Corps for a full two-year term. Tuition support is also available for graduate students. Contact the Peace Corps for more information, or check *www.peacecorps.gov*.

FACT

Some study-abroad programs offer an internship option. If you are lucky enough to find an opportunity that fits your interests and academic background, you may enrich your travel with some actual international job experience. This may not pay money, but if it gives you an advantage over your peers in the job market later, it might be worthwhile, especially if you were planning to travel abroad anyway.

The Woodrow Wilson Foundation

The Woodrow Wilson Foundation hosts a number of internship programs that are related to U.S. government agencies. These internships especially encourage women and ethnic minorities to apply. Most of these internships, including those for the summer, come with scholarships that are enough to fund several years of study. Applicants must apply before the end of their sophomore year to be eligible for three-year scholarship awards or before the end of their senior year to be eligible for graduate school scholarships (which are good for a significantly shorter length of time).

Private Sector Internships

Many international internship programs are sponsored by big business institutions and corporations, such as Proctor & Gamble, Coca-Cola, the Altria Group, and Microsoft, among others. These are sometimes restricted exclusively to students whose goal is to enter an MBA program. In other words, if you want to get one of these internships, it really helps to be a business major. Majors in the liberal arts have countless options in business and government sectors also. Most businesses and government agencies list their internship possibilities on their Web sites under their employment/career links.

Many undergraduate students take advantage of overseas internships with host-country companies. Most of these internships with private sector companies only pay their interns enough of a salary to cover their basic living expenses—which, you should note, does not include the cost of overseas airfare. Do a Web search to find companies offering these internships, using the corporation's name, the word "internship," and your chosen country as search words.

Special Program Jobs

A so-called "special program" job is a lot like an internship in many ways. However, there is one key difference between the two. Although you will often find them through your school, special programs, such as those listed in the following section, have different rules regarding eligibility; eligibility for these jobs is usually not bound by or restricted to the rules and policies of your school. When you leave school or graduate, the program may wish to retain you as an employee if that is what you would like.

Some of these special program jobs even have scholarship availability and internship options once you reach graduate school. The best way to find these jobs is to start by asking questions at your college or university. If the school cannot help you or does not participate in any of these programs, you can search the Web for more information about any specific program (see the following sections for ideas) and for tip on how to apply.

Never sell yourself short by automatically assuming that the only part-time job you can get is in fast food or food service. If that's not what you want to do, keep looking. College students have a number of more professionally oriented job opportunities open to them. Investigate all your options before settling for a part-time job that you hate.

Jumpstart

Jumpstart is a program that recruits college students to serve as part-time members each and every academic year. This is an opportunity for college students to contribute to a public service while they are in school. As a member of the Jumpstart Corps, students work one-on-one with a child. It is the task of a Jumpstart Corps member to help that child build the basic skills needed to succeed in school. In Jumpstart, students also build relationships with local families and develop ties with the community while developing leadership, academic, and vocational skills.

Job Corps

Job Corps has a number of employers who serve as workplace mentors. Both small and medium-sized companies, as well as national companies such as HCR Manor Care, Cisco Systems, and AAMCO Transmissions, are part of the Job Corps workplace mentor team. A number of these participating companies have ongoing partnerships with Job Corps, which helps them to find and recruit entry-level workers. Some other companies have only recently come into contact with Job Corps, hoping for an opportunity to learn about the organization's work-readiness training and intensive career preparation.

Seasonal jobs can be excellent opportunities. College students often fill summer positions as construction workers, painters, and camp counselors. Some of these jobs pay more than other employment options, especially if the student has special skills or experience.

Many of these companies later offer to hire Job Corps graduates. Job Corps provides students the guidance and support they need to secure permanent employment.

Where's the Beef?

Yes, my friends, the U.S. Department of Agriculture wants you! The USDA has a number of student opportunities designed to provide students with academic studies, on-the-job training and experience, and an opportunity to work with the USDA as they are completing their college education. The USDA has programs for both undergraduate and graduate students, with paid opportunities to work as assistants to scientific, professional, administrative, and technical staff members. USDA also has opportunities for grad students to fulfill their career goals through challenging internships that provide the possibility for permanent employment. You can find more information about these possibilities on the Web at *www.usda.gov*.

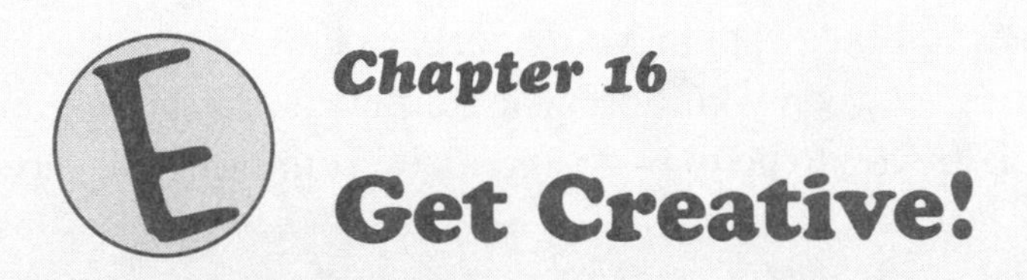

Chapter 16

Get Creative!

Not everybody travels the straight and narrow path when it comes to finding a source of income. In fact, there are those among us who do not travel on a defined path at all. If you refuse to choose security over creativity, and are ready and willing to take risks, this chapter is for you. You have a number of possible options—some are just a little more, shall we say, "unorthodox" than others.

Turn a Skill or Hobby into Cash

Do you have a particular hobby that you really enjoy? Do you love to tend to a nice lawn or know how to care for animals? Are you a talented ballet dancer? You might wish you could be spending more of your time developing your favorite hobby and less time working at a job that just does not excite you (or that you hate with all your heart). Believe it or not, you may not have to choose between your hobby and a paycheck. It might be easier than you think for you to go to work and enjoy your hobby at the same time.

Do Your Homework

When you start thinking about turning your favorite hobby into a source of income, don't forget to do your homework. Always know all the facts before making any choice. Though you might have enjoyed training your puppy to sit and shake hands, you might not be cut out to be a pro dog trainer. Always research the market thoroughly. There may be obstacles along the way that could mean big trouble for you. Whether you plan to start your own full-fledged business, or spend a few hours a week earning a little extra spending money, find out the laws and regulations that apply to you before you start posting flyers.

Different states have varying kinds of licenses for different kinds of jobs. Being your own boss sounds fun—but come tax-time, you may find yourself dishing out even more money to the federal government. As a self-employed person, you must pay the full portion of Social Security taxes (as an employee, you can count on your employer to kick in half). This, plus other taxes and the general cost of doing business, can turn what looked like an easy profit into money and effort down the drain.

FACT

Consignment shops are a great way to sell anything from handmade clothing to artwork such as sketches, sculptures, and paintings. Consignment shops will display your self-made products in a sales environment and pay you for each item of yours that they sell.

Have the Right Attitude!

Successful entrepreneurs are enthusiastic about their ideas and dedicated to their businesses. This sounds simple enough, but it can be a lot tougher when it actually comes down to doing it. To be an entrepreneur, you cannot be the kind of person who has dozens of hobbies and likes to do a little of this and that, here and there, without ever truly committing to any major passion. You must not allow yourself to be distracted, abandoning an idea during development to give attention to the next idea that captures your interest. Successful entrepreneurs are generally committed to perfection and dedicated to achieving their goals. They know how to get going when the going gets tough.

If you do consider yourself the entrepreneurial type, it might be a good idea to take a course or two in business, no matter what your major is. Coming up with ideas will help you put a business together, but it is the little details of the business world that can soon bring your "good idea" crashing to the ground before it has even had a chance to take off.

Start a Business

Not all enthusiastic and dedicated people turn out to be great entrepreneurs, but optimism is essential to even get your idea off the ground. Whether you are the owner of the local news rag or the CEO of a *Fortune* 500 crew, you must be able to see positive opportunities in difficult or negative situations. Without a certain level of optimism, it will prove nearly impossible to motivate your workers, or to keep your business moving whenever times get hard (and, eventually, they will).

Do What You Love

The best place to look for the right business is to look within you. What are your hobbies, passions, and interests? Do you have any specialized skills? What inspires you? What gets you motivated?

Running a business is like carrying a baby all the way to full term and then delivering it. You may be scared of doing it. You might be happy and enthusiastic at certain times, and moody or doubtful in others. And there are going to be times when it is going to hurt . . . a lot! However, there is no going halfway—you are either in or you aren't. Decide before you begin. Being an entrepreneur means having the responsibility to ensure that your business develops and grows until it is able to function without your constant supervision, attention, and intervention. You've got to decide how the business will operate, as well as find a way to control your operations while overseeing them.

Friends Do Not Let Friends Become Their Employees

It is imperative to any small business, or any business for that matter, that the right people are hired to do the right kinds of jobs. Your friend who goes on impulse shopping sprees with credit cards her parents do not even realize she has yet may not be a good choice for a business partner. Certainly don't make her your chief financial officer. Oh, and you know that friend whose back seat is so full trash that nobody can sit back there? He would not exactly be a great candidate for records keeper.

No matter who works for you, if you do have employees, remember to reward those employees who actually work—they can be the hardest to keep around. You may or may not need a partner or other employees in your business endeavor, but if you do, be sure to keep these points in mind.

If you have responsible friends who want to get involved, by all means, let them help. But make that sure you spell out your requirements and expectations clearly beforehand. Both parties must be able to keep in mind that this is a business proposition, and that during business hours, you're employer and employee and not best buddies.

Have a Plan!

Very few of us enjoy making decisions. Decisions mean commitment. Bad decisions lead to problems and can mean losing the respect of one's peers. Owning a business—particularly an undercapitalized startup—is all about making decisions with limited market research and imperfect information. Where should your business be located? Can you do it from your room? Do you need to hire help? How should you price your products? What should be your first target market? One of the main differences between having a hobby and having a business is the need to make real decisions with financial implications. Will you enjoy it?

Money—Ya Gotta Have It to Make It!

Again, depending on your hobbies, passions, and interests, you may need to create a business plan and generate some cash to get started. Once you've written a business plan and established that your hobby can indeed be a sustainable business, the next step is to finance its execution. Unless you thrive on adversity, do not quit your day job (or in your case, college) until you know that you have sufficient money to fund your business plan. Getting financing is not easy and requires personal sacrifice—whether it involves borrowing from your family's savings, your relatives and friends, credit cards, or professional investors. If things do not work out exactly as mapped out in your business plan, will you be able to support a contingency plan to ensure that the business survives? If you do not have the money from your personal network, will you be willing to sacrifice ownership and control to outside investors? Obviously, starting your own full-fledged business is a lot of work. If this sounds like more than you're up for right now, don't be discouraged. There are still plenty of ways you can make money.

Remember that there is absolutely nothing wrong with any job that you finally choose to do, as long as it comes with a paycheck. College is not the time to find your dream job; it is the time to get the education that you need in order to find a dream job *after* you have graduated.

Use Your Skills

Nothing says that you have to go out and try to be the next Donald Trump. Starting your own business might be the furthest thing from your mind. Maybe you're just looking for a way to do what you love while getting paid to do it. Well, aren't we all? Wishful thinking or not, here are a few examples of the kinds of general talents or skills that are in such demand that they have actually pulled in a nice-sized income for many of today's American college students.

Web Designer

A particular computer science major started designing Web pages. He did this in his hometown, and the experience got him one of the best campus employment jobs at his college. He continued to have clients from his hometown who paid him for Web site updates during the academic year. And his college not only gave him a campus job, it hired him to do some additional contract-type projects, too.

Disc Jockey

A lot of college students have collected an arsenal of CDs in their lives and know more than the average Joe or Jane about the world of music. If this sounds like you, then why not make some money sharing your collection of tunes at your college or even community dances, local raves, frat parties, and other events? Students can earn several hundreds of dollars for nothing more than a few hours' work (at least they call it work). Be warned, however, that you must have the personality, the tolerance level, not to mention the variety of music, to handle a job such as this.

FACT

A student who was a 4-H member when she was younger works part-time boarding and training horses in the evenings and weekends. She has been around horses all of her life and is glad to be able to continue her hobby while in college. The hours are perfect for a college student—a couple of hours in the evening and about 8 hours on the weekend.

Jobs for the Active, Outdoor Type

Okay, so you are not exactly computer-savvy—after all, you can barely even get your printer to work, let alone help others with their computer problems. As for being a disk jockey, you were cursed by the heavens with a tin ear. What else can you do? Here are some positions that will put you in the great outdoors.

Referee

This is a great job for athletics-oriented students. If you know a sport really well, consider being a referee for your college's intramural league. Of course, if you are an athlete who knows the sport well, you would probably rather be playing in the league—but refereeing is going to pay you money! Contact some of the local coaches of your sport, or the person in charge of intramural sports to find out what possibilities there are for you in this area.

You can improve your odds of landing a job such as this even more if you have some kind of official certification. Some students become licensed officials in order to referee elementary and junior high games for local teams (which pulls in a lot more money than one might think). Sometimes, basketball coaches can earn several hundred dollars on a single Saturday for refereeing games at a tournament.

Lawn and Yard Work

Exactly where do the professors run off to during those summer months? Some of them stay in town. Of course, there are also a number of them who go away for the summer in order to carry out research projects, supervise travel-study trips, or simply to take a vacation from students. It would be rather lucrative to be the sole proprietor of your own low-price lawn care business. That's right—when in doubt, underbid the professionals. Professors who need someone to mow the yard and trim the shrubs while they are away would make a great clientele platform. Who knows? Once they see what a good job you do, some of them may decide to let you come over all year round.

Providing Service with a Smile

Maybe nothing is sounding good to you yet. You're the type of person who just wants to be social, someone who wants to help people out. Don't worry, you're bound to find something right up your alley, too. Just ask yourself these two questions: "What can I do to help people?" and "What kind of help will they pay for?"

House or Pet Sitting

Speaking of professors being away for the summer, do not forget all those empty houses and lonely pets—professors will also be looking for pet and house sitters. Many people who have pets are left with no option but to put them in a kennel or leave them with friends or relatives whenever they leave town. If only there were a student who would go to the pet owners' homes and baby-sit their pets, walk their dogs, or whatever else needs to be done in the owner's extended absence.

Can I get paid to go on a cruise?
Yes! Some cruise lines hire college students for jobs during their busy seasons. It is hard work, though—sometimes ten hours a day and six days a week, and you probably will have to share a room with another student worker.

Babysitting

Houses and pets are not the only things that need to be cared for on occasion. If you like children and have experience babysitting, then consider getting involved in child care. Think of how many professors, administrators, and staff members have children. If you can establish yourself as a responsible, caring babysitter, you can have all the work you want. You might start by creating flyers or asking your own professors if they know of anyone who needs a babysitter. Chances are they will jump at the chance of hiring a distinguished, intelligent, role-model of a student such as you to watch their kids. People in the community may be interested in hiring you, too, especially if you are working on an education or child-care degree.

Hair Styling

Okay, maybe not necessarily "styling," but how about hair cutting? This is a business that at least one or two students at every campus seem to create to help pay their bills. If you have any experience in cutting hair, you have a ready-made business. After all, how often does the average student need a haircut? And how often do most students go home to visit their own hair stylists? In most cases, the time periods are not going to match up. Students will need haircuts more often than they can get home to get them. You are the answer! Just charge slightly less than the going rate in your area, and keep those scissors sharpened. You will be one busy, scissors-happy student.

Travel Service

If you take a vehicle with you to college, consider giving rides to students who live in your hometown area. Usually, they will pay top dollar to get home. Parents usually kick in too because it saves them a trip. Other students need rides to airports, or even weekly trips to the local grocery store or pharmacy.

Be a Guinea Pig

You might be able to pick up some quick cash by answering a twenty-page questionnaire or tasting a dozen different new flavors of soda. Upperclassmen and graduate researchers sometimes look for students to participate in their research projects. They might offer $20 to come for a psychology experiment of an hour of listening to people's recorded laughter and then answering some questions about how that experience made you feel. You are likely to be able to report that it made you pretty happy . . . to have an additional $20 in your pocket!

Make Money Writing

English majors, listen up! This is a great job for your field of study. When a lot of people think about being a writer, they think of names such as King, Grisham, or Crichton, writing novels of hundreds of thousands of words and making millions on royalties alone! Okay, chances are that this is not going to happen. Hey, then again, it might! But in order to make money as a writer on a regular basis (or at least regular enough to pay the bills), you need to set your sights just a little lower.

If you like to write, consider a part-time position with the local newspaper. Many newspapers hire interns and part-time writers. It could give you valuable experience if you want to pursue this kind of a career.

Keep It Simple

Know your strengths and weaknesses. Are you really good with descriptive language and love to write depictions of your environment and places you have been? If so, start writing articles to submit to travel magazines. Are you an experienced martial arts enthusiast? Then articles on martial arts might be your ticket to a steady paycheck. Whatever you decide to write on, try to choose something that is a part of your regular routine, or at least something that is a regular part of your life. Writing articles requires you to be able to churn out several pieces a month, which means you need a wide range of things to write about. If you can't pump out work, you will not make much. But hey, if you love writing, just do it anyway as a side thing!

Keep It Freelance

Freelance writing can be a really great way to work for college students who love to write. The number-one reason might be that they cannot fire you! As a freelancer, you are not actually an employee. Sure, you can lose work here and there, but there are no early-morning staff meetings or editorial bawl-out sessions to deal with. Freelance writing work is low stress, low maintenance, and very low drama. Of course, it can also be very low pay, depending on who your employer(s) are.

Paying Work Is Best

When faced with a choice between covering the school production of *Streetcar Named Desire* for $50 and spending all night with a chatty, middle-aged woman who wants you to write her memoirs for free (of course, she says she will pay you once the book gets published!), go for the money. Unless you get one of those gut feelings that you can't ignore, always go for the paying jobs first. This should be done for several reasons, the most important one being that you need the cash. The other reasons are that paying jobs look good on a writer's resume compared to pro-bono jobs, which mean nothing to publishers or almost anyone else in the industry.

Chapter 17

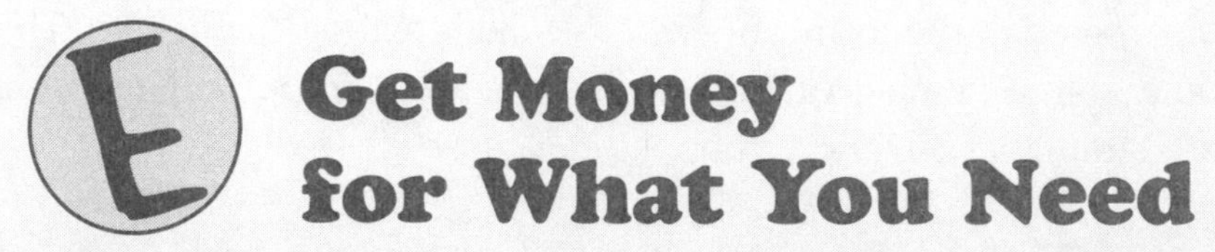

Get Money for What You Need

It is true that you can't always get what you want. However, it is also true that if you try, you can get what you need. As with everything having to do with finding money and resources to pay for an education, the main question isn't whether there are resources to be found, it's whether you have the drive to keep on searching until you find them. Do not get discouraged if you are turned away a few times. Keep on pushing on.

Textbook Vouchers

As you have already seen, the high and rising costs of college textbooks is one of the biggest financial burdens for anyone trying to acquire a higher education. However, even with textbooks, there are options that a student can choose from to help ease that burden just a little. The main way to get help comes in the form of what are called textbook vouchers. These can come from a number of different sources and can put a major dent in the cash strain that buying your books can cause.

There are often no rules forbidding students from posting flyers to sell their textbooks themselves. Hold on to your textbooks until the next semester, and then post them at a few dollars less than what the bookstore is charging for the used version of that book. You are almost guaranteed to get more for it than you would have from the bookstore.

How to Get a Voucher

Textbook vouchers are offered by some institutions and organizations. These vouchers are given only to those students who have been approved for financial aid, and they are accepted only during specific times of the academic year. In some cases, the vouchers are automatically offered as part of the financial aid package for needy students. In other cases they may be part of an academic or athletic scholarship, or they may be a completely separate scholarship.

Once they've been awarded, textbook vouchers can normally be obtained at the institution's campus business office. Students who use vouchers should plan on having about $300 or more at the beginning of the college year for their textbooks. Student supplies such as notebooks, pencils, computer disks, and blue books may not be purchased with textbook vouchers. You don't get cash back from a voucher purchase, and they will be accepted for the total amount of the textbook purchase only.

Focus America, a nonprofit organization in New Jersey, has a program for high school and college students in which they volunteer thirty hours of service in exchange for a $50 textbook gift certificate. A program such as that benefits you in two ways: you can obtain volunteer work experience, which is great for your scholarship applications and resume, and you earn a voucher toward your book costs.

There are a number of outlets available now on the Internet to help students sell, buy, and swap used textbooks. Most often, these sites provide a better deal to students than just selling textbooks at the campus bookstore. Check out *www.half.com* as well as *www.amazon.com* and that old favorite, *www.ebay.com*.

Refund Checks Can Be Vouchers, Too

Students who have financial assistance credit balances left over (in amounts that are sufficient to purchase textbooks) may charge those books against their credit balance. For example, let's say you had $8,000 in scholarships and financial aid allotted to you for the year, and your total tuition turned out to be around $7,500. That would leave you an extra $500. You would then be able to charge your textbooks toward that extra money. You just need to request a refund check/textbook voucher in the amount of the balance from the institution's cashiers' office. These vouchers are also sometimes available at the university bookstore. Different schools have different policies on when this money can be made available, so this option is not always convenient for everyone.

Are Vouchers Always Good for Students?

There is a downside to the voucher system, mainly because it restricts the student's choices as a consumer. With a voucher, you have no choice but to get your books from the campus bookstore. So if you find a textbook for a better deal at a different bookstore, you don't have the option of paying the lower price for the book. That's because book vouchers can only be used at the university bookstore. For example, a book used for two semesters of a humanities course might cost a student $75. However, the same text is also available at an online retailer, in used but acceptable condition, for only $20. A student with a textbook voucher has no choice but to pay the $75 for a new text from the campus store or maybe $50 for a used one (if they even have any used books left). Either way, the student is not getting as much bang for a buck, voucher or no voucher.

School Supply Freebies

Outside of tuition and books, one might think that there are few other expenses to be concerned with. However, items such as paper, pens, pencils, folders, floppy disks, and blue books can start to add up not long into the semester. At any exams, without failure, there will always be that one student at the classroom door who is panhandling for a blue book or even a pencil. Most people think these students are just unprepared for class. The truth is, most of them are so broke they could not even afford the couple of bucks it takes to pull one of each of these items together at the last minute. That's pretty sad, isn't it?

Shop with a friend and buy in bulk to save money. Ramen noodles cost only pennies a package when you buy a whole case. The same savings apply to school supplies. Split value packs of pens, notepads, or whatever else you need.

Are Supplies Qualified As Tax Write-Offs?

In a word, "No." In most cases, expenses for textbooks and school supplies cannot be used for tax credits such as Lifetime Learning (described in Chapter 3). They are also not qualified under the new tax breaks for higher-education expenses. However, if a student is required to directly pay the institution for certain supplies, meaning that buying those items is a requirement under the student's enrollment or admission, those items would then qualify as valid tax-deductible expenses.

Around Town

Here is a universal truth—if a big name organization, company, or other group is handing out free promotional items, people are going to take them. These handouts increase a company's overhead, and its marketing department will likely request a bigger budget the following year, but smart businesspeople simply do not care. Why? Because if some moocher has a cupful of pens with that company's logo on it sitting on his or her desk, then to the businessperson, it was money well spent. Pens have a tendency to switch owners a few times before they finally make it into the wastebasket. Students always have a use for pens that still work. To the broke students, free pens can be almost as good as free food.

FACT

One excellent way to get money for what you need is to hold a garage sale and sell the things you do not need. If you offer to pick up discarded items from relatives and friends too, you will have more to sell, and you will help them out by hauling their unwanted items away.

Are you skeptical about the truth behind the "freebie" mentality? Perhaps you think the freebie always comes with a catch. If so, answer this question—if freebies don't work as a promotional tool, then why are there so many Web sites online devoted to advertising and offering them? When a company offers free stickers at a Web site, the intention is to attract loyal site roamers to send an e-mail asking for some. The company then has another address to use when they send out e-mail advertising. Once the foolproof solidity of this idea was realized, everybody and their CEO started using "specialty advertising" freebie offers on the Web.

On the Web

To find freebies and/or freebie-specific Web sites, start by opening your favorite search engine and doing a search for "cheap free school supplies." You will immediately see just how many options there are online. This is not exactly the fastest way to locate the specific type of "freebie" that you are in search of, but it is a good way to start. Just don't get distracted by the offer for 1,000 golf tees (with Joe's Roadkill Shack advertisements on them) while you are doing your search. As you look around, anyone and everyone you run into is going to try to get you to take something and, if you like, take anything you want that's offered—so long as you do not lose sight of why you started searching in the first place.

Redistributing the Wealth

The National Association for the Exchange of Industrial Resources (NAEIR) offers aid to supplement tight budgets for a number of nonprofit organizations by way of their somewhat unusual membership program. NAEIR collects donations from overstocked inventories from big and small American businesses, and then they redistribute these goods to their members. Over the span of a quarter century, NAEIR has pulled together and redistributed goods donations worth more than $1.6 billion.

Members of the NAEIR simply pick what they want from a catalog that they receive five times throughout the year. Once members make a selection, they pay for the shipping and handling costs. NAEIR members pull in an average $18,000 worth of supplies a year. However, memberships to the NAEIR are not free, and you must represent a legitimate nonprofit organization. (By the way, student organizations and clubs are considered nonprofit.)

Students should never miss the opportunity to get free school supplies. Many local businesses also try to attract new students as potential customers by offering things they will find useful. Take what you are given, but be sure not to sign anything resembling a contract. You might get duped into more than you bargained for.

Financial Aid to Buy Your Own Computer!

A free computer? Sounds good, doesn't it? It is a very real possibility, though one that's somewhat little known and that rarely gets taken advantage of by most students. Remember that each institution creates its own budget, or total cost of attendance, for students. The cost of attendance is the maximum in financial aid that any student can receive from all available financial aid resources. That means the total package can include scholarships, grants, loans, and so on. Any of these can be used to help students buy their own personal computers. "But," you say, "don't most schools now have computer labs that are open for student use at no cost?" Yes, they do. However, please read on before dismissing the great advantage of having a computer at your own exclusive disposal.

Computer Labs Can Be a Pain

Most colleges and universities have computer labs where students who do not have their own computers can go to do assignments, write papers, check e-mail, and so on. If you walk into one of these computer labs, you are likely to see many students using the machines. This is an arrangement that works very well for a lot of students. Very few institutions actually require students to have their own computers, so do not feel that you have to make that major purchase if you are someone who does not mind using the lab computers for free. (Just remember that sometimes all of the computers are being used, and you might have to wait in line to access one.) If the school you decide to attend says that you *must* have a computer of your own, or if you think it is necessary to have your own, then consider investigating the college's policy regarding computer costs.

FACT

Some universities have begun to offer waivers of out-of-state tuition increases for students who qualify for the school's honors program. This means that a high GPA and an excellent academic record can do more than just help you get into a good college; they can also help you get money to pay for it.

Federal Regulations Can Help

Federal regulations allow a financial aid office to add the cost of purchasing or renting a computer to your official cost of attendance. Institutions are not required to add this expense to the cost of attendance, but most will. If the institution does allow for this expense, then the cost of the computer must be documented with the financial aid office. Usually the purchase can be in the name of the student, student's spouse, or student's parent, as long as it is intended for the student's educational use. Allowable expenses include the computer hardware, printer, and necessary software.

The government allows schools to set their own policy and maximum allowable amounts, so there is some variation in policies among institutions. One institution might allow a one-time $1,500 increase to the cost of attendance for the purchase of a computer. Another institution might allow $2,500, allowing a student to request $1,300 as an entering freshman, for example, and another $1,200 as a rising senior.

How This Works

Suppose a student enrolls at a college that allows a $2,000 one-time-only computer expense, and that the institution's policy states that the purchase must be made no sooner than June (if you entered the college in August) and that receipts are required. If you were able to borrow enough money from grandma to purchase a computer after July 1 for a cost of about $1,800, then submit the college's computer expense form, along with receipts, the college would increase your cost of attendance budget by $1,800. (You can't get more money back than the computer actually cost). This means that students are eligible to receive an extra $1,800 in financial aid. Of course, eligibility does not mean that you will automatically receive the additional money. It just means that you now have "room" to accept that much more financial aid. If nothing else, you can at least take out a low-interest alternative student loan (and remember—pay back your grandma!).

Many states have an office of vocational rehabilitation, which may provide educational assistance to disabled students. Funds may be available to help cover costs of special-needs items, in additional to tuition, fees, books, transportation, and personal expenses.

Other Aid for Textbooks or a Computer

Federal financial aid is not the only way to get vouchers for your textbooks or money for a computer. Loans, certain scholarships, and a number of grants can and will help out with the high prices of textbooks and computers. For example, any surplus on tuition aid can more often than not be used toward your textbooks or other educational expenses. Take a look at some of the following examples. Even if you don't see anything that directly applies to your situation, ask your particular financial aid source whether there is money available that you can use toward textbooks and other supplies.

Use Your PLUS Loan

One thing that a number of parents have begun to do is to charge the cost of their student's personal computer to their credit card, and then submit the receipts and forms for the purchase(s) to be included as a part of their PLUS loan. Once the student's entire tuition bill is paid off in full for that academic year, any excess funds that have been created from the PLUS loan can then be refunded so that the parent can pay off credit card charges for the computer.

Use Excess Scholarship/Grant Money

The really fortunate students who have more scholarship money and grant assistance than they know what to do with can purchase a personal computer with these excess funds. All they need to do is follow their institution's procedure for increasing the cost of attendance, then accept another scholarship or grant for up to that allowable amount. Again, you would have to find a way to pay for the computer up front (out of your own pocket), or charge it to a credit card, until they receive a refund/reimbursement check for the cost after the tuition account is paid off by the scholarship/grant funds. Now that's a pretty awesome way to purchase your own personal computer without putting a permanent dent in your bank account!

Where to Ask

If getting help to buy a computer might be of interest to you, it is suggested that you inquire at your college or university about their specific policy for student purchases of personal computers. More often than not, this information can be extremely difficult to locate on an institution's Web site. Colleges usually don't publicize such benefits at all. This means that if you don't ask, you won't ever know if you could have taken advantage of this opportunity.

FACT

Some students with financial need can qualify for state programs that will lend help for the purchase of certain grocery items or other essential things. Every state's program is (of course) different, just as every student's situation is unique. If you think you might qualify and are interested in finding out what might be available, contact your local state assistance agency.

Alternative Spring Break

Spring break is a time to party for many college students. Money is the last thing on many students' minds as they head in the direction of sunny beaches and a week of nothing but good times! Sounds good, right? You bet it does, but spring break can also turn into a very expensive week. Take care not to fall into the trap of blowing all of your hard-earned cash (or worse yet, make the mistake of charging your trip on a credit card) for a luxury experience that you know you cannot afford. Why not investigate alternative, more cost-efficient spring break trips? Many colleges now offer these trips as a part of their service work programs.

For example, you might sign up to volunteer with a group such as Habitat for Humanity. Habitat for Humanity even lets you travel for free, just as long as you commit a certain number of service/volunteering/work hours while you are at your chosen destination. This is an option that could involve some hard work, which may not sound as appealing as a care-free week of soaking up some rays on the beach, but you will be able to save a ton of cash and end your spring vacation with the feeling of satisfaction in knowing you have helped those less fortunate than yourself. Each college or university will have its own program requirements and budgets for these kinds of programs, so the number of hours required and travel expense compensation will vary from school to school. However, if you enjoy service work, this could be a great opportunity.

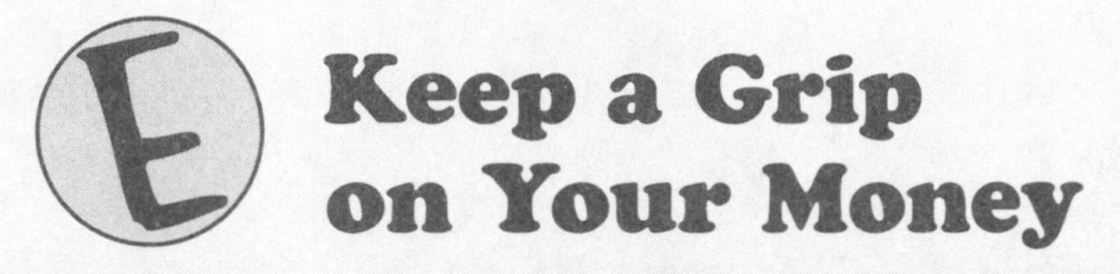

Chapter 18

Keep a Grip on Your Money

Money can be a lot like food—when you have enough to eat, it seems as though there is plenty of it, so you just eat as much you want. However, when your cupboards start to look bare days before your next scheduled shopping trip, you start to regret your previous overindulgence. Use money as you should use food—as you need to. Don't spend if the situation isn't a necessity, and always be sure to have some in reserve for when times get rough.

Keeping a Budget

A big part of being able to pay for college has to do with the student's ability to live economically and think frugally. Keeping a budget is a good habit to get started on early. The reason a budget is so important is that it lets you know exactly how much money you have coming in and where certain portions of it will have to go. That means you can wonder, "Do I have enough money to go out dancing with my friends?" and be able to check your budget to find the answer.

Rule Number One—Follow the Budget

A budget that is written down but ignored is completely worthless. If you do not stick to your budget, it completely defeats the purpose of having one. Sticking to your budget will aid in preventing you from making the all-too-easy mistakes of overspending, "accidental splurging," or (heaven forbid) sending too much money for a bill, or (even worse) sending the wrong check for the wrong bill. All that fun and excitement you're having can come to a screeching halt when the $200 you were supposed to give to a roommate for rent "accidentally" got spent on a night out with some friends.

QUESTION?

What makes a good budget?
Here are some qualities of a good budget: accurate income projections, inclusion of expenses that don't happen every month (such as auto repair and income taxes), tracking and recording of spending, and a line item for savings. A good budget should also give you a meaningful picture of where your money goes and where you might be able to cut costs.

Rule Number Two—There Are No "Accidents"

Nobody "accidentally" spends money. That would be physically impossible. The only thing even remotely close to accidentally spending money is having it stolen. The truth about these "accidental" situations is that the spender was not keeping tabs on the finances. You may say, "I thought I had more money in my account." Think what you like, but remember that the bank is going to charge overdraft fees regardless of what anyone thought.

If you find yourself feeling uncertain about how much money you have and whether it is okay to spend it, then you should pick from only one of two possible options. The first option is to verify your balance by balancing your checkbook and checking your records against the bank's. Most banks offer account services over the phone or Internet, making it easy to know how much you've really spent. Be sure to take into account an estimation of any checks you have written lately that may not have cleared. Once you know how much is in your account, you can decide whether spending is a prudent choice. The second option is simple—you can just wait and come back when you know you have enough money (this is probably the best option, anyway). There is no third choice. (If you think the third choice is to ignore the budget, you need to go back to rule number one.)

The basics of budgeting are the same for students as they are for anybody else: list the sources of your income, such as savings from your summer jobs, financial support from your parents, financial aid from the school, scholarships, and income from your job (if you have one). Then list your expenses, such as tuition, books, groceries, gas, entertainment, and so on.

Rule Number Three—Never Break Rule Number One

The best way to keep a budget is in advance. When you receive a paycheck, go ahead and write out any and all expenses for that pay period. However, just because you have money left over does not mean you should feel free to go out and spend all of your surplus cash. Once you have accounted for your expenses, the best thing to do is to cut that amount in half. This remaining amount should be allotted for spending or what some people refer to as "walking around money," and the other half put into either a savings account or other investment plan (such as a Section 529 plan).

Convenience Versus Frugality

Convenience is a funny thing, and it is often surprising how much people are willing to pay for it. For example, an express train ticket might cost $15 for an hour's journey. However, you could also take the local and make several connections for only $3 each, for a total trip of two hours. That's $9 the long way with a couple of inconvenient connections, and $15 for the short and easy way. Honestly, which one would you choose? Most of us would choose the express. Why? It is faster and more convenient. However, sometimes frugality means sacrificing convenience to save a little cash. Some day, you may find yourself in a situation where the long, inconvenient way is the only way that you can afford to get to where you are going.

Bicycle Versus Car

No, "bicycle versus car" doesn't mean finding out who would win in a game of chicken. It just means that if you have a car, you might be tempted to drive from one place to another on campus. While that is a lot quicker and more comfortable than slinging the twenty-pound backpack over your shoulder and huffing and puffing up and down hills (not to mention dealing with inclement weather), it costs you money. If you think of the gas money you would save, in addition to the obvious health benefits of walking or riding a bicycle, you may want to let the car sit in your parking space until you really need to drive some distance. Better yet, just bring a bicycle and leave the car at home with your parents. Then you won't have to pay for gas or a parking permit.

Use coupons. Coupons can save you a lot of money when you buy groceries and other necessities. In addition, restaurants often run specials and promotions that make it affordable to go out to dinner once in a while.

Cafeteria Versus Fast Food

Your school dining hall may not have the best food in the world, exactly, but if you have a meal ticket, you should use it. Not using it is just as good as flushing money down the toilet. If the dining hall is open, and you have paid to be on the meal plan, then it is a waste of money to eat out. This does not mean you can never eat fast food or go out to a restaurant—just don't do it every night. Going out to eat all the time can be a very easy habit to fall into. To motivate yourself to stay on campus, try dividing the cost of your meal plan by the number of meals it covers. Thinking of each skipped meal in terms of actual dollars may help you realize what a waste of money it is.

Super-Sizing Means Too Much Food and Money

Why just get the regular combo meal when you can super-size it? Come on, who among us really eats that many French fries or drinks that much soda (before it goes flat and gets watered down by melting ice)? Very few of us do. Super-sizing is something that fast food corporations thought up to get customers to spend an extra fifty cents or so on more fries and few extra ounces of soda, all of which adds up to about a cost of a few pennies for them.

The truth is, you are better off just getting the combo. If you're still hungry after that, order a little something extra. This will cost you less over time than just super-sizing all your meals because you think you are getting a better deal. You actually might be getting more for your money, but the extra fries you pay for will often end up being thrown in the garbage, along with that flat soda you could not bear to finish.

If your expenses are less than your income, you are in good shape as long as you stick to your spending plan. If your expenses are *more* than your income, you need to find ways to cut spending or increase your income.

Curb Impulse Buying

One of the biggest threats to a student's finances can be the pitfall of impulse buying, which is the rampant spending of money with little or no regard for any kind of planned budget. These impulse spenders often spend money that they do not have, or they spend money faster than they can earn it. Either way, this is a really fast way to dig yourself into a deep financial hole. Develop some method to curb spending impulses—if not one of the suggestions given in this book, then something else, just as long as it works for you.

The Twenty-Four-Hour Rule

The twenty-four-hour rule is a good one to follow. Basically, it means that you start out by planning all of your purchases in advance. Then, if you see something that you'd like to buy but have not planned on buying (meaning it is not figured into your budget), then you have to wait a minimum of twenty-four hours before actually forking over any cash. You may wonder how this can do any good. Often when we first see something we want in the store, we are excited, enthusiastic, and acting on the adrenaline/endorphin rush we get from that impulse. Waiting a day to buy something gives that rush some time to wear off. Maybe after that much time, you will realize that it wasn't such a good deal after all. You may also find out there is something else you want even more that you couldn't have bought if you'd chosen to go with your impulse.

FACT

In addition to being creative in finding income to pay for college, you may also need or want to get creative in where and how you receive your higher education. Not everyone attends a traditional four-year residential college or university. Don't forget about career and vocational schools, two-year degree programs, community and junior colleges, and institutions that have part-time, evening, and distance-learning programs available.

Leave Your Card At the Dorm

Being able to resist just whipping out that magic credit card every time you see something you want can be a lot easier than you might think. The most foolproof method for doing this also happens to be the easiest method—just leave the credit card in your dorm room! Walking around with a loaded credit card can be very dangerous. Keep yourself free and clear of trouble by leaving the plastic somewhere other than in your wallet (such as a strongbox, a locked drawer, or a safe).

The best thing about cash is that everybody accepts it! Of course, most businesses are set up for credit transactions because they are more common. However, sticking to cash is a good way to avoid spending more money than you actually have. Once all of your cash runs out, so does your ability to keep spending.

Cheapskates 101

Penny pinching is more than just an anal-retentive tendency—it is a way of life. There is nothing wrong with being the kind of person who sees a pen on the ground and picks it up to see if it is still good. There is also nothing wrong with going through the pizza sample line at the grocery store a second time. Are you a cheapskate? If so, stand up and be proud of who and what you are! If not, consider the following pointers, and maybe you can become one, too.

Free Toiletries

There is no reason to let yourself become the Stinky Steve or Nasty Nancy of your dorm hall. Toiletries are always available; you just have to know where to look. If you are an athlete for your institution team, for instance, you will likely have a number of opportunities to stay in hotels. Some members of clubs and organizations also have opportunities to travel. Hey, those toiletries come with the cost of the room, so grab up all that you can—soap, toothpaste, shampoo, conditioner, and any other hygiene product you can find is free game. Just don't go crazy and start raiding the housekeeping cart in the hall. Taking what you paid for is one thing—flat-out stealing is wrong.

A student who lives in an off-campus apartment may be able to get a discount on the cost of rent if paid in advance for the whole semester or entire year. Ask your landlord or property manager.

Dollar Stores

Dollar stores are awesome! Yes, you do sometimes have to sacrifice a certain level of quality if you buy things there. However, it is always better to have a cheap version of a necessary item than not have it at all. If you want to pay a dollar for each item, then be sure that the store is actually a "dollar" store, not one of those stores where everything is just dirt cheap. For example, Dollar General is not a dollar store; it is a store where things are "generally" a dollar. The Dollar Tree, however, *is* a dollar store. Everything's a Dollar is also a dollar store, because, well, everything is actually a dollar. Of course, if you have no other options, Dollar General will do.

Thrift and Outlet Store Clothes

Don't worry—going to a thrift store these days does not necessarily mean being limited to shopping at the local Goodwill. In fact, outlet malls as well as clothing stores such as Ross, TJ Maxx, or Marshalls have made bargain-hunting for brand names somewhat of a hobby for the American shopper. Paying a fair price for nice items is no longer a practice restricted to the extremely poor.

Clothing is something you need, but you don't necessarily *need* brand names. While some students like the crisp, preppy look of expensive and fashionable designer label clothing, there are plenty of other students who are completely comfortable with the idea of purchasing certain items at secondhand or discount stores. Not only does this idea appeal to those who are frugal at heart, it also gives students an opportunity to express themselves through one-of-a-kind creations that cannot be found in today's trendy stores or high-dollar fashion catalogs. Of course, this may or may not be your cup of tea, but for many money-wise students, the idea of getting their clothes at a fraction of the cost is very appealing.

Free Fun

Where is it written that enjoying yourself involves spending money? Many people do not take advantage of the activities available to them every day, especially those that cost little to absolutely nothing. Sometimes we just do not realize that these options even exist. For some, we would often rather complain about having nothing to do (really our excuse for being lazy). Here are a few good examples of stuff to do that costs nothing or next to nothing. There is an endless amount of other options, and they stop where your imagination does.

Go to the Park

Public parks can be a great place to spend a cheap afternoon walking, cycling, inline skating, or just lounging under a tree looking for pictures in the clouds. Take a couple of friends and a Frisbee, and you'll be set for the afternoon. Before you head out, however, it is a good idea to ask your resident advisor or another student who has been around for awhile to find out if a park is safe, or if there is a safer time to go.

Not all parks are safe once the sun starts to go down. Before you check out a park in person, you would be wise to call the local police department to ask about problems they may have, and to find out if there is a park curfew (a ticket for this, believe it or not, can run you as much as $90 or more).

Card Games

Spades, Go Fish, Old Maid, Slap Jack, and even solitaire are all card games that are fun and generally known to most people. Even if you cannot find anyone who knows how to play one of these games, they are relatively easy to teach. Some students bring a deck of cards with them to school for something to do on a rainy day (or when they are broke). Even if you do not have a deck of your own, either the dormitory or the student commons often has a gaming area where you can sign a deck out with your student ID card. If you do not know how to play any of these games, you may want to learn a few before you get to college.

Unorthodox Card Games

Welcome to the world of action-card gaming. These days there are a number of somewhat unorthodox card games on the market, and you would be surprised how many college students play them. Magic, The Gathering, Pokemon, Dragon Ball Z, Duel Masters, and a number of other trading-card games are popular just about anywhere you go. The nice thing about these card games is that once you know how to play one of them, you have the ability to play just about all of them. The basic game play stays out the same way, and it is just the terminology of the items that changes.

Attend Free Events

If you are bored, all dressed up with nowhere to go (that you can afford), and broke, then attending campus or community-hosted activities can be a great alternative to doing nothing at all. Even if you are not broke, you should attend some of these events—school administrators often determine the budget for student activities by looking at how many students attend these hosted events or participate in on-campus activities. So, if you want your school's student activities department to offer more or better stuff, then you should help them out by attending at least a few events a semester.

Community Events

Outdoor festivals, flea markets, and other local events are fun and often charge no admission. Does the local community host an annual pig-calling festival? Do they have a fall pie-eating contest? Find out. Often enough, events such as these get posted in a section of the university newspaper or monthly student activities calendar (if your school has one). Don't be a stick in the mud. Expose yourself to a new community by attending events such as these—the stories that come out of them make for great ice-breakers when meeting new people!

If you need something to do and don't want to spend money, there are always plenty of places where you can volunteer your time. Local YMCA or YWCA, Red Cross, day care centers, and retirement communities would be delighted to have the assistance. You would keep a hold on your money *and* do something good for your local community.

Guest Lectures

Each year, the administrators of colleges and universities spend a fortune trying to attract scholars, writers, thinkers, and sometimes even celebrities to giving lectures or seminars. However, fewer students are regularly taking advantage of this opportunity than did in former years. Sometimes, institutions do not actively promote these guest speaker lectures due to a limited amount of seating, which they fear might cause a problem with overcrowding.

However, most schools do have an available schedule of expected speakers with a description of their backgrounds, an announcement of when and where each lecture will be held, as well as what subject the speaker is covering. This is a great opportunity for college students. It can offer you a broad range of exposure to some very interesting and brilliant personalities in today's world—politicians, authors, columnists, and the experts in their fields of study are all examples of the types of people who are on the college lecture circuit each year. These days, for example, former president Bill Clinton is paid big money to speak at American universities, as are scholar authors such as Dr. Evans Lansing Smith, former Texas poet laureate James Hoggard and his wife, linguist Dr. Lynn Hoggard, as well as popular celebrities such as reality TV cast members and real-life heroes.

Free Campus Activities

Campus recreation or some other form of student activities department often hosts free on-campus (and sometimes even off-campus) events for students. All you need in order to get through the door at one of these activities is your student ID. Second-run (sometimes first-run) movies, intramural sports, hosted games, social events, poetry readings, ethno-cultural festivals, and a number of other events and activities are often made available to students every week throughout the academic year. Get out there, and get involved!

Chapter 19

E Don't Let Credit Cards Destroy You

There is not very much of a gray area when it comes to credit cards. Nine times out of ten, credit cards are either your saving grace or your worst nightmare. However, this is not to say that there isn't a gray area in which credit cards are simply a part of daily life. There is such an area—but only a very small number of people actually manage to stay inside of it. This chapter is meant to help you identify the good, the bad, and the ugly sides of the credit card world.

Preapproved? Don't Fall for It

Everyone has received one of those jubilantly designed letters marked "Important Credit Information Inside," or something to that effect. When you open it up, what's inside? That's right, a "preapproved" credit card, with "magic" credit. Be warned. Cards like this are mailed out by the hundreds of thousands each year to first-year college students. These students have no credit, and therefore do not have "bad" credit. However, seventeen- to nineteen-year-old students who have no concept of how money works can get themselves into some serious financial trouble with cards such as these, where all they have to do is dial a number, answer a few questions, and Shazam! They have a shiny new card that will buy them anything up to the credit limit.

Credit Is Not a License to Spend!

Having a credit card does not mean you have a green light to immediately max it out. Credit cards were designed to give you a little extra spending power when you *need* it! This does not include using the card to buy things that you cannot afford or to live a frivolous lifestyle that is far beyond your means. A good rule for using credit is to use it when you *have* to. For example, when the car you use to get to work and school breaks down, you can use the card to pay for the repairs which cannot afford at the moment. (Just to clarify, a running car is a necessity; a completely new wardrobe is not.)

FACT

Using credit cards is not always a bad decision. They may offer very low rates—sometimes even zero percent for a period of time, with no annual fee. However, paying off this debt before the interest starts to accrue or increase is absolutely essential.

Bad Credit Sticks Longer Than Superglue

Seven years! That is how long it takes for a bad credit report to be wiped from your record! This means that foreclosures, surrenders, and repossessions of any kind will be there on your credit record for the entire world to see for no less than seven years. This can even have an effect on your ability to get a job, especially if you want to work in jewelry, management, or security occupations.

Why would bad credit keep a person out of a job? And why single out people in jobs having to do with jewelry, management, or security occupations? Well, for those jobs you almost always have to be bonded (a type of insurance that protects the employing company for losses in the case that you turn out to be a thief). For a bond, they do a credit report check, and if you have what they deem to be too much bad credit on your credit report, that bond can be next to impossible to get. No one wants to have someone with financial troubles handling too much cash or highly valued items. Sure, you are allowed to put your own comments/explanations on your credit record—but it probably won't do much good.

It can be a real pain, but you should always read the fine print. If you find something you do not understand or that concerns you, go to a professor, a lawyer, or a parent to have them explain it. Don't call the credit card company for an explanation—not unless you want them to give you a sugar-coated and misleading answer designed to get you to see things their way.

Interest Rates and Fees

The annual percentage rate (referred to in most paperwork as the APR) can usually tell you how much interest you are going to pay on the balance of your credit card. However, keep in mind that this does not include fees and charges that are outside the category of interest. There may be so-called "hidden fees" that are kept from your attention with that low interest rate dangling there in front of your eyes. In addition to comparing the interest rates of different cards, watch for the ones that include these annual fees or other hidden costs.

Many cards offer low introductory APRs. Be sure you know how high the interest rate will rise after the introductory rate expires. Two cards that seem to offer the same terms may actually end up costing you quite different amounts in the long run. This is another perfect example of why reading the fine print on your credit card agreement is so important.

Credit card companies will often drastically raise their interest rates (sometimes to as much as 24 percent) after a customer makes a certain number of late payments. Read the fine print and know whether the payment is considered posted on its postmark date or on the date it reaches the bank or the credit-card company. Unfortunately, once you accrue a few late payments, the credit-card companies can start charging you the inflated interest rates for as long as you have the account.

Variable Rates and More

A credit card company might choose to use a variable or a fixed rate to charge you interest. This can have a significant effect on what you end up paying just to use your card. Credit card companies using variable-rate plans base the fluctuation of rates on set indices. Often they will use the prime rate, one-month, three-month, or even the six-month treasury rate. If not, they will likely use the federal funds or federal reserve rate, also known as the "discount" rate. Most of this information can be found in the money or business sections of major newspapers.

Fixed Rate Plans

Take a close look at fixed-rate plans. They may be a couple of percentage points higher than a variable rate; however, you do get the advantage of knowing that your interest rate will not change without your knowledge. Variable rates are exactly what they say they are—variable. This means that they change, up or down. You take your chances with a plan like this.

If your rate is fixed, however, there is a piece of legislation called the Truth in Lending Act that requires the lender to provide no less than fifteen days' notice before increasing your interest rate. In certain states, laws require credit card companies to give you even more advanced notice. Some financial analysts argue that since a fixed rate can be increased after a fifteen-day notice, this plan is not all that dissimilar from a variable plan, which is subject to change at any time with no prior notice. The difference is that if you are notified of the change, you will potentially have the chance to switch to a new card before the changes take effect, if you so desire.

When you are trying to choose between two credit card offers, look closely at both plans. If you decide to choose a variable-rate card, find out if there are caps on how high or low your interest rate can be. For example, if the lowest variable rate possible on one card is 17.5 percent, and rates are currently going down, choosing another option might not be such a bad idea.

How can I protect myself from identity theft?
Some credit card companies are now willing to offer you a protected guarantee in the case that you become another faceless victim of Internet fraud or identity theft. This kind of protection plan is referred to as an Internet fraud guarantee, and it is a good thing to take advantage of whenever it is made available.

Paying Dearly

No matter the plan you choose, accept the fact that you are going to be making monthly payments. Each credit card company has its own way of determining your monthly minimum. Some companies start by calculating the interest rate. Once the interest rate is figured, the credit card issuer then adds a number of percentage points (the margin, as it is called) to this rate to come up with what the consumer will be charged.

Sometimes they choose to use a different formula to determine the rate charged. For this, they usually multiply the rate by a certain number that they refer to as the "multiple" (no one really knows how this number is decided on, save the ones who come up with it), or they add the rate to the margin and then multiply by the multiple. Confused? Don't worry. All you really need to know about the monthly payment is that you need to pay it, and that this is the *minimum* you should pay each month. (More on this later in the chapter.)

Stay Under the Limit

Getting yourself over a credit card's maximum limit is like digging yourself a ten-foot-deep hole. Instead of climbing out when you had the chance, you paid no attention to how deep it was getting and just kept right on digging while you were still in it.

You see, once you break a credit card's maximum credit limit, the fact that you are no longer able to use the card may be the least of your problems. At that point, the credit card company does one of two things. If you have been a good customer and always make your payments regularly and on time up until now, they might raise your limit. (This may be more convenient for you, but it is dangerous because it makes it extremely easy for you to get yourself into even more debt.)

Be sure to pay all your bills on time. If you live in an apartment, this includes your rent and utility bills. If you own a car, it could include your car or insurance installment. In addition to maxing out your plastic, late payments are another way to ruin your credit.

The second thing they might do is much worse (and kind of underhanded when you think about it). Some credit card companies penalize their customers with an over-the-limit fee, which is charged each month until the customer gets back under the limit. It can be as much as $20 (on top of the interest you are already paying). Suppose you are planning on paying your card's minimum, "low monthly payment" of $40 a month. You are $200 over your credit limit, with a balance of $2200 at 10-percent interest—you can be in some serious trouble. From the $40 you decide to send in, the company first deducts the "over the limit" fee of $25, which leaves only $15 that goes toward your actual payment. If your interest is 10 percent on a balance of $200, then your interest alone is $22! You haven't even paid that off for the month, let alone started paying off your actual purchases!

If this is the way you pay your bills, your balance will not go down—in fact, it will go up! That leftover $15 from your payment will be deducted from your interest of $22, roughly leaving an unpaid amount of around $7. Well, guess what? Your balance is now $2207! That's right! You sent the credit card company the minimum $40 monthly payment, and you are now in rougher shape than you were when you started. Even worse—you are still over your limit, which means the same thing will happen next month. You are paying them regularly, but your balance just goes up and up.

According to the federal reserve, consumer debt hit $1.98 trillion in October 2003, up from the $1.5 trillion reported in 2000. (This figure includes credit card debt and car loans, but does not include mortgage debts.) This report showed that credit card debt alone was at $735 billion, with the average individual cardholder's outstanding balance at about $12,000. Kind of scary.

How to Get Back on Top of Things

At this point you may be wondering how in the world you would ever be able to get yourself back under the limit once you've gone over it. If the balance continues to go up, how do they ever expect anyone to pay it off? The truth is that they don't want you to pay it off. They're happy as long as you just keep on sending monthly checks while they let your debt keep on rising.

Of course, the best thing for you to do is not use your card to make charges that you know will exceed its set limit. You should also never allow yourself to use credit cards as a way to live in a style beyond your financial means. Use your credit card as an alternative to cash when necessary (for example, reserving a hotel room often requires a credit card), not as a substitute for money you do not (and will likely never) have. If you stick to this basic philosophy, then you should have little to no trouble being able to pay off your monthly credit card balance.

However, if this advice comes a little too late for you, don't despair. There is a way to get your balance back down below your credit limit. Unfortunately, the hard truth is that once you reach this point, you are going to have to shell out some major cash to get things back under control.

Don't think that running up credit card debt will help you qualify for more financial aid. Consumer debt due to lifestyle choices is not taken into consideration when financial aid is determined.

Get It Over With

The first choice is to find a way to pull together enough to pay down your balance to a point well under the credit limit. In the example we used earlier, this would mean the $207 that you're over your limit, plus another $25 to cover the next month's "over the limit" fee, and another $22 to cover interest charges.

In order to get yourself back under your maximum credit limit, you would have to make a single payment of $255.08. (That's an additional 25 percent on top of how much you went over your limit. See how those credit card companies get you?) If this is your method of choice, you're going to have to take a deep breath and just write the check.

A Bit At a Time

Your second choice is to cancel the card and pay off the balance a bit at a time. (Once you have canceled the card and charges have ceased, this can be as little or as much as you are able to pay each month). If you do this, it is imperative that you do not get another card! Believe it or not, the credit company will try to get you to take another one once they have you back under the limit.

Minimum Payments Will Get You Nowhere!

The third choice is definitely the worst. In fact, it's not even an option but an example of what not to do. Just keep paying minimum monthly payments and let your balance continue to go up. This is not exactly among the wisest of decisions, but plenty of college students still opt for it.

Most cards, including Visa, Discover, and MasterCard make it very easy for you to follow this third path—be aware of this so you can avoid paying them forever. These cards offer what is known as revolving credit. This means they let you carry a balance, which they charge interest on (they call these finance charges). They will also require you to make a minimum payment. The minimum payment is commonly around 5 percent of your balance or $10, whichever is highest. Your payment varies depending upon your balance, the interest rate, and the method by which your finance charges are being calculated. As you learned above, if you only pay this minimum payment, your balance is more likely to continue to rise than to start going down.

FACT

Some credit cards, such as American Express, require you to pay off all of your charges each month to avoid being bombarded with penalty fees. As a benefit, they usually have no finance charge and sometimes no maximum limit. However, there are sometimes annual fees in order to use the card.

"Rule of Three" and Building Good Credit

The "Rule of Three" is a fairly foolproof and easy plan to follow. Basically, it governs the number of credit cards you can have. Your best bet is to start off with only one card. If you want to get a different card, with a higher balance, lower interest rate, or promotional offer, that's fine. However, if you insist on having multiple credit cards, never have more than three.

Start with One Card

The best thing to do, especially while you're in college and still learning about credit, is to limit yourself to one card. If you have a $1,500 balance on one credit card with a 7-percent interest rate, it will not be nearly as complicated to pay it off as the same total debt spread out over three different credit card companies—$500 on one card with a 10-percent interest rate, $500 on another card at 12 percent, and $500 on a third card charging 7 percent. The best way to start out is with only one card and then to wait a year or two while you build up a good credit record.

Pay for Purchases Immediately

Later in life, there are going to be things that you will need and not be able to afford to pay in full. When this time comes, you do not want to have the credit mistakes of your past coming back to haunt you. (Remember that bad credit sticks around for seven years). However, to start out on the right foot on your credit report, here is a tip—go ahead and get a credit card, but do not use in the usual fashion.

Here is how it works. First you need to save up enough actual money to buy a relatively expensive item (such as an MP3 player or digital camera). Once you have that money in the bank, write out a check for that amount, paid to the order of the credit card company. Put the check in an envelope, address it to the credit card company, and make sure you have a stamp on it. Now go to the store and purchase the item on your credit card. As you are driving home, drop the envelope in the outgoing mail. By doing this, you will never have to worry about your balance getting out of control, and you will build strong credit.

If you have bad credit, and know that you have bad credit, be very wary of any guaranteed offers for credit approval. Operations such as these take advantage of those who cannot get credit elsewhere. Unfortunately, the price of approval is often an interest rate of over 20 percent.

Stories Bill Collectors Tell

Credit problems in recent years have actually resulted in fatalities. Credit woes have been responsible for the deaths of a number of college students who were unable to cope with rising maxed-out balances, harassing phone calls from bill collectors, and the stresses of work and school. Some students were so upset and harassed that they committed suicide, seeing no other alternative way out of their situation. Don't let this happen to you. Be aware of some of the little white lies that the credit collectors like to use.

First and foremost, you cannot go to jail for not paying your credit card bills! No matter what a bill collector tries to tell you, this is simply not true. All that the credit card companies can really do is screw up your credit report or be a pain in the rear by sending bill collectors after you. These collectors will start calling you at all hours of the night (sometimes even calling at work, trying to get you into trouble with your boss in an attempt to intimidate you into paying).

Secondly, the credit card company is not going to take you to court and sue you! That's another tall tale that bill collectors try to use to scare unknowing young cardholders into paying their outstanding balances.

Lastly, they cannot take your automobile from you as compensation for unpaid debts! This is almost a half-truth—you could lose your car if you bought it with your card and can't pay it off. But it's not the credit card company who can take it from you. Until it is paid in full, when it belongs to you, that car belongs to the institution that loaned you the money to buy it, whether that's your credit union or the car dealership. This means the dealership has the right to try to repossess it—not the credit card company. Bill collectors do not have the power or legal right to seize it, or any other piece of property that you have, regardless of what the self-important telephone tough guy from the collection agency tries to make you believe. The only power that credit companies have to enforce collection of outstanding debts is to write bad things about you on your credit report. End of story.

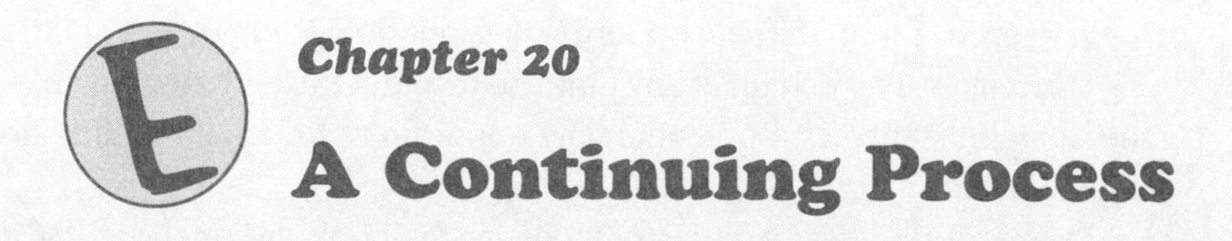

Chapter 20
A Continuing Process

No matter how successful you have been at preparing yourself financially and finding ways to pay for college, you should brace yourself for the continued diligence it is going to take to renew existing financial aid each year and to find additional sources of assistance. Families realize that the student must invest an immense amount of time attending class, studying, and doing homework. Don't short-change yourself by failing to recognize that both students and parents will need to continue to invest time on the financial part of this endeavor as well.

Always Keep Searching!

Many families make the easy mistake of thinking that everything that can be done regarding college financial aid (all the paperwork, confirmation corrections, and other assorted details/red tape necessary to receive financial aid) must be completed early. It is true that early awareness and planning help keep you from missing opportunities, but do not forget that additional opportunities may pop up at any time. Be resourceful, and investigate every new circumstance as a potential new opportunity for acquiring additional financial aid.

Many of the ideas and instructions in this book are intended for high-school students. However, you should always keep in mind that no matter what stage of the college process you are in now, you should be continuously researching to find out about the financial aid or scholarship/grant opportunities presently available. Scholarships and new financial aid programs are created all the time, but it is up to you to stay on top of them. How will you know what's new out there if you just stop looking?

Potential outside sources of scholarships or grants include professional organizations, community clubs and organizations, corporations, unions and trade groups, nonprofit foundations, and religious organizations. Look both in your local area and nationally for these opportunities.

Going Through "Major" Changes

Every new circumstance you encounter or new experience you become involved with has the opportunity to offer you hope by opening the doors to new financial aid possibilities. For example, if you for whatever reason decide to change your major (or minor), you may be able to apply for a scholarship now that was not available to you before. As a business administration major, liberal arts scholarships were not open to you. Let's just say that while you are taking a required English course, you suddenly discover that you absolutely love mythological studies. You decide right then and there to change over to a liberal arts major. Suddenly, those liberal arts scholarships that were out of your reach before are now wide open for you to start applying for.

The Door Swings Both Ways

Despite the fact that a new major can open up paths for new financial aid opportunities, remember that this is a door that swings both ways. Even though you may have gained scholarships and financial aid possibilities by picking a new major, you have also cut yourself off from those resources that were available only to students in your former major.

Along the same lines, if you started out in an associate degree program at a two-year institution, but you change your goals and decide to go to a four-year college or university, you may be eligible to receive new grants or scholarships. But there may be other kinds of aid for which you will no longer qualify.

It's Never Too Late!

Until a college student actually walks across the stage and receives a Ph.D., it is never going to be too late to keep an eye out for new ways to help him or her pay for the cost of a higher education. Here is a list of a few last-minute solutions for prospective college students as well as their parents. These methods may be able to help you in dealing with these somewhat time-sensitive financial aid/scholarship/grant moments:

- Talk to your high school guidance counselor about any remaining possibilities you may still have.
- Pool together whatever financial resources you can (that means it is time to call in some favors, if you have any owed to you).
- Assess where you are financially.
- Figure out your financial boundaries, and recalculate exactly what you will need to be able to afford college.
- Contact the financial aid office at the colleges you are considering and ask what is still available.
- Apply to some additional colleges if you still have the time. (Remember that other institutions may still have financial aid

available, even if you are already too late to get aid at your original college of choice.)

FACT

College scholarships are often made available to students through their high schools. Students who are still in high school should try to become as familiar as possible with their high school guidance counselors. All students, and even parents, should make frequent visits to the guidance counselor's office.

What to Do If You Missed the Deadline

Is it already too late for you to make the deadline for this year? Has the "last minute" already lasted a minute? Has the opportunity for financial aid come and gone, leaving you coughing on the dust of its wake? Do not fear, dear friends. Even though it may not make you feel any better right now, there is always another chance to reapply next year (or, sometimes, even next semester). Instead of beating yourself up over what a pickle you feel like you have gotten yourself in, start taking the initiative now to make the most of the situation.

The first thing you need to do is find out what deadlines you have already missed. Be sure to mark them down for next year so that you don't miss them again. Now remember that a year can be an awfully long time for you to hold onto (and keep track of) something, so be sure that you store a list of these dates in a place where they will not only be safe from destruction (doggy teeth, baby hands, and so on), but where they will not be forgotten between now and the time you need them. Also file any paperwork that you have already started so this will be handy when you're ready to officially restart the application process.

So You Missed the Boat

As you sit waiting for the next year to roll around, be sure you don't waste that time sitting around, twiddling your thumbs and staring at the ceiling until you think you see faces in the spackle patterns. You could at least find a full-time job and start working on some extra savings to help pay for your tuition. However, if you're still set on getting started with your education, you do have a few remaining options. You might want to think about considering a deferment of your enrollment until the second (spring) semester, or perhaps you could postpone your enrollment until the following academic year. This will still allow you to go to your chosen school, and it may give you the financial aid you need to afford it.

Be sure to always make, file, and keep copies of any paperwork having to do with your financial aid. Applications, essays, letters of approval/award, and other important documents should all be duplicated.

Consider Community College

Another last-minute option to consider is enrollment in a few core requirement courses at a low-cost institution such as the local community college. By doing this for a semester or two (or even three), you give yourself some transferable course credits, along with enough extra prep time to plan more for your academic future. You will also be able to avoid missing the boat when the next financial aid application deadlines roll around.

Important Tips

College is expensive, no matter who you are or what your financial situation. The best thing you can do to maximize the ways you pay is to remember that nobody else is responsible for finding that money and placing it in your lap. It is up to you to research your options, complete the forms, and do any follow-up work. Help is available through your high school guidance office, federal and state agencies, college financial aid offices, loan officers, and friends who have been through the process before, but students and parents themselves must work together and take the initiative. Every student's situation is unique, and the most qualified person to help you is you!

Never Dismiss an Opportunity

Finding money to pay for college is not something you should wait to do until a week before classes begin. You need to start early and keep searching throughout your college years for opportunities to obtain, earn, or save money. Do not look only for scholarships. Other kinds of aid are often just as good (and remember that some people use the terms scholarships and grants interchangeably). No- or low-interest loans can also help you pay for college.

A wise person once said, "It is okay to borrow money if it will help you make money later." If you apply yourself in college and pursue a career that you enjoy, the borrowed money will feel like a good investment once you have the job of your dreams. Work opportunities are another thing to consider while you are in college or between semesters. Besides helping you earn money for college, they can sharpen your job skills, provide valuable experience, and give you something to put on your resume.

FACT

Some types of aid are guaranteed, or automatically renewable, while others require you to apply again. Be sure to know which types of aid you receive require a renewal application. College could cost a lot more the next year if you give up thousands of dollars by not making that new application for certain types of aid after they have expired.

Do Not Get Discouraged

You may find that you have exhausted all possible sources of aid, but don't give up! Budget an hour or two every week to continue to investigate your options. At some point, whether it's a week or a month later, you may discover a new scholarship opportunity. Also, as you progress in your major and advance in class level, other possibilities may become available. Free money is the best way to pay for college because you don't have to pay it back, but don't forget about ways to save or earn money. Not spending money unnecessarily, for example, is an effective way to free up money to pay for college.

An education is something no one can ever take away from you! Very few people who have graduated from college regret the sacrifices it took for them to acquire their education. It is a goal worth sticking to, and for most families, the joy of seeing their graduate accept a college diploma is one of life's greatest thrills. Just keep working hard, continue searching for ways to pay for college, and keep your eyes on the prize at the end. Your accomplishment will be even sweeter for knowing that you did not give up.

Know All the Facts

It is a jungle out there, and it is easy to get lost in all the terminology and paperwork. But don't be intimidated! You can find out what you need to know if you invest some time and ask questions. Use the experts at your disposal, both in your high school and at the colleges you visit. Write down the important information. You may understand it at the time but find that you are confused later. Detailed notes will help you understand what you forms you need to complete and by what due dates.

When you decide on a college, remember that many people out there are willing to work with you to help you succeed. You are definitely not alone. Whatever questions you have, or difficulties you encounter, whether they are academic, social, or financial, people are ready to help. They will do as much as they can to answer your questions and to let you know your options. Think of your parents, admissions counselor, academic advisor, financial aid administrator, and other key people in your college experience as partners in your education. If you work together with them, you can find your unique pathway through your education and enjoy one of the most rewarding experiences possible.

No matter what kind of career you plan to pursue, you need to be sure to take the suggested prerequisite high school and college courses in the basic areas of math, history, science, English, foreign language, and other core requirements.

Brace for the Unexpected

Always remember that no matter how prepared you think you are, you can't plan for everything. This is something for both parents and students to understand because unexpected circumstances can and likely will happen. Most of these unforeseen circumstances revolve around a single universal truth: Things change! Permanence is a word—nothing more.

"What kinds of things can change," you ask? Well, take a look at just some of the possibilities:

- **Majors**—It is common for all students to change their major focus of study at least once, if not more often, during their college careers. Just because you choose a major in advance does not guarantee that this will be the degree you will graduate with.
- **Minors**—These, too, are known to change.
- **Goals**—Yes, they may be called "four-year" institutions, but that does not guarantee a degree in four years. Understand that a student's first and last year should have lower class loads than the middle two (or three) years.
- **Relationships**—Break-ups happen (even if both parties left home for the same university). Pregnancies happen, boyfriends/girlfriends quit school and join the Navy, and so on.

These life events/choices could affect your college education, and parents at least should brace for them. However, as a parent, you also need to understand that if one or more of these occurrences takes place, what your student will need (more than anything) is your encouragement, love, and support. Try to keep the amount of chastising to a minimum, as too much lecturing about all the "should haves" and "could haves" (along with the occasional "why didn't you") might not only alienate you from your student but cause him or her to lose hope when he or she needs it the most. Be there for your children. They need you—whether they are willing to admit it or not.

Appendix A

Financial Aid Glossary

academic year:
An institution's educational time period, consisting of one twelve-month year, the academic year usually begins in July and ends in June. The year is divided into standard academic terms of quarters, trimesters, or semesters. Each institution must designate whether its summer term is considered as the beginning or the ending of the academic year.

accrual:
The accumulation of interest, usually applied on a monthly basis. Some educational loans, such as the unsubsidized Stafford loan, allow for regular payment of accrued interest, so the loan balance remains at the principal amount until the student enters repayment.

adjusted gross income (AGI):
This amount is calculated on a tax filer's federal income tax return. It is the taxpayer's income minus certain allowable amounts, such as student loan interest.

American College Testing Service (ACT):
A nonprofit organization that does research and provides assessment testing for educational purposes.

amortization:
A loan's repayment is scheduled over a specific period of time, during which the principal decreases, or amortizes. Payments include both principal and interest.

assets:
Generally speaking, assets are owned items that can be converted into cash. When completing financial aid applications, be sure to understand which assets must be reported and which should not be included. For example, when completing the FAFSA, the value of a family's primary residence is not counted as a part of the parents' or student's total assets.

assistantship:
This type of financial aid is usually provided for graduate students. It waives all or a portion of the student's educational expenses in exchange for teaching, assisting, or involvement in research/experimental work.

balloon payment:
A large payment used to pay off 100 percent of the remaining balance of a loan. This is an option with certain educational loans.

base year:
On financial aid forms, the tax year that is used to determine how financial aid will be made available and/or awarded. Usually refers to the calendar year prior to the one in which the student will attend college.

bursar:
A treasurer or business officer at a college or university.

campus-based programs:
Federal financial aid programs for students that are managed by the institution. The institution determines eligibility and distributes award amounts. Current campus-based programs include the Federal Supplemental Educational Opportunity Grant (FSEOG), federal work study, and the federal Perkins loan program.

capitalization:
A term for interest that accumulates on top of already unpaid interest. If a borrower pays off the interest on a loan as it is accrued, there is no capitalization.

CSS profile:
A financial aid application created by the College Board, a national non-profit association.

commuter student:
A student who lives with one or both parents, or some other relatives, while attending college courses.

consolidation loan:
This type of loan combines two or more educational loans into one new one by paying off the original debts and creating one new, larger one in their place.

cost of attendance (COA):
The estimate of a student's educational expenses for an academic period of time. The costs generally included in a student's cost of attendance are as

tuition, fees, room and board, books, transportation, and personal expenses. Institutions may also include additional items. A student's total financial aid package is not allowed to exceed his or her cost of attendance.

custodial parent:
For financial aid purposes, the parent with whom the student lived with for the most time during the past year. If the student did not live with any one parent more than the other, then the parent who provided the highest amount of financial support is considered the custodial parent. If the custodial parent has remarried, then the new spouse is also required to provide financial information that will be included in the calculation.

default:
Failure to repay a loan according to the legal agreement originally signed by the borrower. Default status appears on the borrower's credit report and can prevent further loans from being granted.

deferment:
A legal postponement of an individual's obligation to pay back a loan. Many educational loans are automatically deferred until the time a student graduates from college or ceases to be enrolled as at a least half-time student.

delinquent:
A debtor who has failed to make a loan payment by the required due date. Usually a late fee is assessed, and the borrower has a certain amount of time to make the required payment before the loan is considered to be in default.

demonstrated financial need:
Usually the difference between the student's cost of attendance (COA) and the expected family contribution (determined through the FAFSA). A student's demonstrated financial need will not be the same at every college and university, mainly because the cost of attendance varies.

dependency status:
Students are considered either dependent or independent in terms of their eligibility for financial aid. Status is determined based on a number of criteria, including age, number of dependents, and military service.

disbursement:
Money paid out on behalf of the student. Financial aid is usually disbursed in equal parts over the course of the academic year (as in once a semester).

endowment:
The property or funds that provide an institution of higher learning with a permanent source of income. Some colleges and universities have endowed scholarships, which are funded with the earnings or interest of a donor's monetary gift to the school.

entitlement program:
This is a type of financial aid that guarantees all eligible students will receive the authorized amounts (because they are "entitled"). The Pell grant program is one example of an entitlement program.

expected family contribution (EFC):
The amount of money that the student and family are expected to pay toward the student's educational expenses over the next academic year. It is determined by a formula developed by Congress, called the federal methodology.

Federal Application for Student Aid (FAFSA):
A financial aid application form provided by the U.S. Department of Education. It collects income and asset information of the student and student's parents (if the student is dependent). Most institutions require that students complete the FAFSA in order to be considered for financial aid.

Federal Family Education Loans (FFEL):
The "umbrella" federal loan program that includes federal Stafford loans (whether subsidized or unsubsidized), federal PLUS loans, and federal consolidated loans. Borrowers of loans that fall under the FFEL are required to apply through private lenders, and the federal government guarantees the loans.

federal methodology:
The mathematical formula, developed by Congress, used to calculate a student's expected family contribution (EFC).

federal Pell grant:
A grant entitlement program provided by the federal government for undergraduate students with financial need.

federal Perkins loan:
A low-interest, campus-based loan program for both undergraduate and graduate students. Federal Perkins loans are subsidized, and the repayment interest rate is set at 5 percent.

Federal Parent Loan for Undergraduate Students (PLUS Loan):
A federal loan program specifically designed for the parents of college students. The PLUS loan program has a variable interest rate, which is capped at a maximum of 9 percent.

Federal Supplemental Education Opportunity Grant (FSEOG):
A campus-based program provided for undergraduate students who have an exceptional amount of demonstrated financial need. Priority must be given to Pell Grant recipients who have the highest demonstrated financial need.

federal work study:
A campus-based program for undergraduate and graduate students who have a demonstrated financial need. It provides part-time employment with an hourly wage. Students are encouraged to work in jobs related to their specific academic program of study.

fellowship:
A type of financial aid, usually awarded to college graduate students, that provides for an allowance or cash stipend for the purpose of funding a student's special focus of study.

financial aid officer (FAO):
The administrator at a college or university who is primarily responsible for interpreting and implementing financial aid regulations, policies, and programs.

financial aid package:
The combination of all the financial aid options available to the student for the academic year. Additional sources of financial aid may be incorporated into a student's financial aid package throughout the academic year.

forbearance:
A temporary or complete discontinuance of the repayment of a loan (often by the borrower). Some educational loans have possible forbearance options if they occur under certain circumstances.

grace period:
The time after a student graduates, or ceases to be enrolled in courses as at least a half-time student, before the student must begin to make repayment of a tuition loan.

grant:
A type of gift aid that does not need to be repaid, usually awarded on the basis of need and sometimes on the basis of an applicant's skills, accomplishments, or some other qualifying criteria.

guaranty agency:
The organization in each state that administers the FFEL (federal family education loans) program in that state.

institutional student information record (ISIR):
An institution's version of the student aid report, or the response from the federal processor after a student has filed the FAFSA. Only institutions listed by the student on the FAFSA will receive an ISIR.

interest:
The amount that accrues at a set percentage rate on the amount originally borrowed (the principal). The interest paid on a loan is the amount is costs to pay the loan back (that is, the amount it cost to borrow the money in the first place). Interest must be paid to the lender, along with the principal amount that was borrowed from the lender.

loan entrance and exit counseling:
A requirement for some educational loans to inform the student of a loan borrower's rights and obligations. Institutions can provide this counseling by providing information sessions, one-on-one counseling, or through an online counseling program.

National Student Loan Data System (NSLDS):
The database of borrower information for federal loans, including outstanding balances, status of loans, and disbursements made. The information comes from institutions, guaranty agencies, and the U.S. Department of Education.

outside scholarships:
Scholarships that are provided from a source outside of the institution the student attends.

packaging:
The determination a financial aid administrator makes concerning a student's financial aid eligibility for various types of aid. Packaging can be done through a computer program or manual calculations.

personal identification number (PIN):
A unique identification number that serves as a student's or parent's electronic signature on the online FAFSA. A person's PIN can be used to access other federal financial aid information online and to electronically sign other documents.

promissory note:
A legal document that lists the borrower's conditions and terms of a loan. It includes both principal and interest information, as well as provisions for deferment and cancellation.

satisfactory academic progress (SAP):
An institution's standard of progress, which is required for continued participation in a number of educational programs. It must include a quantitative component and a qualitative component (that is, how many classes the student is taking and the grades being earned).

student aid report (SAR):
A report that summarizes the student's data inputs as recorded on the FAFSA, lists the student's EFC, and may provide further information or instructions for the student.

subsidized loan:
A federal student loan for which the U.S. government pays the interest while the student is enrolled in college courses as at least a half-time student.

tax credit:
A dollar-for-dollar reduction in the amount of tax obligation that can be deducted directly from the amount of taxes the individual owes.

tax deduction:
Expenses that can be subtracted from taxable income (as figured on state and federal tax returns), thus lowering the amount of tax owed.

tuition payment plans:
A program that enables a family to make regular, periodic payments toward any of a student's educational expenses that are not covered by financial aid. This type of plan may be offered by the school or by a private lending institution.

unsubsidized Stafford loan:
A federal student loan that accrues interest in the same way as any other type of loan.

verification:
A process that compares the student's FAFSA information with the student's and the parent's tax return information as well as certain other submitted documents. Colleges and universities must verify students who have been selected by the CPS (central processing system).

verification worksheet
A form that families must complete for the financial aid verification process. This worksheet is provided by the institution and collects necessary information to be compared to a student's FAFSA as well as other verification materials.

W-2 form:
A statement of the wages that an individual earned during the previous tax year. This form is required to complete all tax returns as well as the FAFSA.

Appendix B

Further Reading on Paying for College

A Is for Admission, by Michele A. Hernandez.

The Best 351 Colleges, 2004 Edition, by Robert Franek.

The College Board College Handbook 2004: All-New Forty-first Edition. Published by the College Board.

The College Board Cost and Financial Aid 2004: All-New 24th Annual Edition. Published by the College Board.

The College Board Scholarship Handbook 2004. Published by the College Board.

The College Board Index of Majors & Graduate Degrees 2004. Published by the College Board.

College Admissions Trade Secrets, by Andrew Allen.

Colleges That Change Lives: 40 Schools You Should Know About Even If You're Not a Straight-A Student, by Loren Pope.

The Fiske Guide to Getting into the Right College, by Edward B. Fiske and Bruce G. Hammond.

The Fiske Guide to Colleges 2004, by Edward B. Fiske.

Greenes' Guides to Educational Planning, by Howard Greene and Matthew Greene.

Harvard Schmarvard, by Jay Mathews.

How to Go to College Almost for Free, by Ben Kaplan.

The Insider's Guide to the Colleges 2004: 30th Edition. Yale Daily News.

On Writing the College Application Essay, by Harry Bauld.

The Pocket Idiot's Guide to Surviving College, by Nathan Brown.

Scholarship Almanac, 7th Edition. Published by Peterson's.

The Scholarship Scouting Report: An Insider's Guide to America's Best Scholarships, by Ben Kaplan.

The Unofficial, Unbiased Guide to the 328 Most Interesting Colleges 2004: A Trent and Seppy Guide, by Trent Anderson.

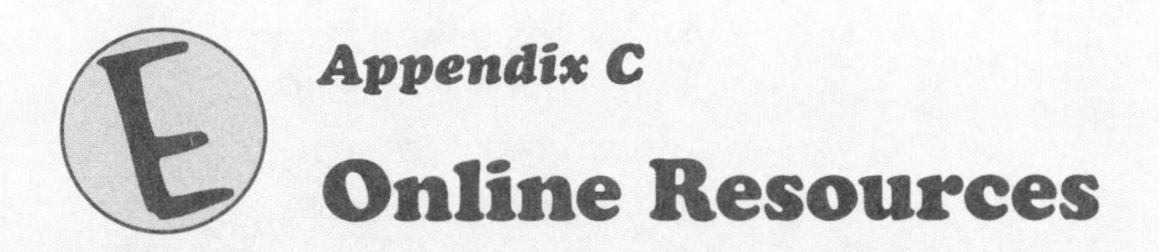

Appendix C

Online Resources

College Search Web Sites
- *www.studentaid.ed.gov*
- *www.embark.com*
- *www.collegenet.com*
- *www.mapping-your-future.org*
- *www.pheaamentor.org*
- *www.petersons.com*
- *www.gocollege.com*
- *www.fastweb.com*

Textbook Sources
- *www.amazon.com*
- *www.half.com*
- *www.textbookx.com*

SAT/ACT Information and Tips
- *www.collegeboard.com*
- *www.act.org*
- *www.review.com*
- *www.petersons.com*
- *www.secretsstudyguide.com*
- *www.sat-secrets.com*
- *www.number2.com*
- *www.collegeboard.com*
- *www.testprep.com*
- *www.mcps.k12.md.us*
- *www.powerprep.com*
- *www.4tests.com*

Planning for College
- *www.adventuresineducation.org*
- *www.review.com*
- *www.collegeispossible.org*
- *www.studentaid.ed.gov*
- *www.fastweb.com*
- *www.focusamerica.org*
- *www.gocollege.com*

College Comparisons
- *www.usnews.com*
- *www.overview.com*
- *www.earnmydegree.com*
- *www.campusdirt.com*
- *www.go4college.com*
- *www.collegeview.com*
- *www.campus-resource.com*
- *www.onlinecollegereviews.com*

Military Service and Department of Veterans Affairs
- *www.military.com*
- *www.va.gov*
- *www.vetfriends.com*
- *www.1800goguard.com*
- *www.usmc.mil*
- *www.goarmy.com*
- *www.army.mil*
- *www.aerhq.org*
- *www.army-tips.com*
- *www.af.mil*
- *www.airforce.com*
- *www.navy.mil*
- *www.asvabprogram.com*

College Savings Information
- *www.collegesavings.org*
- *www.collegesavings.com*
- *www.upromise.com*
- *www.babymint.com*
- *www.moneycentral.msn.com*

- *www.finaid.org*
- *www.americanexpress.com*
- *www.metlifebank.com*
- *www.savingforcollege.com*
- *www.nysaves.org*
- *www.scholarshare.com*
- *www.brightstartsavings.com*
- *www.independent529plan.org*
- *www.usfunds.com*
- *www.microinvesting.net*

Budgets, Debt Management, and College Loan Repayment

- *www.erieri.com*
- *www.mapping-your-future.org*
- *www.ccsintl.org*
- *www.cc-bc.com*
- *www.creditstaff.com*
- *www.youcandealwithit.com*
- *www.nfcc.org*
- *www.center4debtmanagement.com*
- *www.creditreport-net.com*
- *www.debtms.com*
- *www.cs-america.com*
- *www.ammend.org*
- *www.consumerdebtsolutions.net*
- *www.consumercredit.com*
- *www.debtindex.org*
- *www.reclaimmayday.org*

Tax Credit Information

- *www.ed.gov/inits/hope*

Selective Service Administration

- *www.sss.gov*

Social Security Information

- *www.ssa.gov*

Internal Revenue Service

- *www.irs.gov*

Corporation for National Service

- *www.cns.gov*
- *www.americorps.org*

National Collegiate Athletic Association

- *www.ncaa.org*

National Junior College Athletic Association

- *www.njcaa.org*

U.S. Department of Education

- *www.ed.gov/finaid.html*
- *www.studentaid.ed.gov*

FAFSA on the Web: Application and Information

- *www.fafsa.ed.gov*

A

B

C

D

E

F

Q

R

S

Everything® Kids' Bugs Book
Everything® Kids' Christmas Puzzle & Activity Book
Everything® Kids' Cookbook
Everything® Kids' Halloween Puzzle & Activity Book
Everything® Kids' Hidden Pictures Book
Everything® Kids' Joke Book
Everything® Kids' Knock Knock Book
Everything® Kids' Math Puzzles Book
Everything® Kids' Mazes Book
Everything® Kids' Money Book
Everything® Kids' Monsters Book
Everything® Kids' Nature Book
Everything® Kids' Puzzle Book
Everything® Kids' Riddles & Brain Teasers Book
Everything® Kids' Science Experiments Book
Everything® Kids' Sharks Book
Everything® Kids' Soccer Book
Everything® Kids' Travel Activity Book

KIDS' STORY BOOKS

Everything® Bedtime Story Book
Everything® Bible Stories Book
Everything® Fairy Tales Book

LANGUAGE

Everything® Conversational Japanese Book (with CD), $19.95
Everything® Inglés Book
Everything® French Phrase Book, $9.95
Everything® French Verb Book, $9.95
Everything® Learning French Book
Everything® Learning German Book
Everything® Learning Italian Book
Everything® Learning Latin Book
Everything® Learning Spanish Book
Everything® Sign Language Book
Everything® Spanish Grammar Book
Everything® Spanish Phrase Book, $9.95
Everything® Spanish Verb Book, $9.95

MUSIC

Everything® Drums Book (with CD), $19.95
Everything® Guitar Book
Everything® Home Recording Book
Everything® Playing Piano and Keyboards Book
Everything® Reading Music Book (with CD), $19.95
Everything® Rock & Blues Guitar Book (with CD), $19.95
Everything® Songwriting Book

NEW AGE

Everything® Astrology Book
Everything® Dreams Book, 2nd Ed.
Everything® Ghost Book
Everything® Love Signs Book, $9.95
Everything® Meditation Book
Everything® Numerology Book
Everything® Paganism Book
Everything® Palmistry Book
Everything® Psychic Book
Everything® Spells & Charms Book
Everything® Tarot Book
Everything® Wicca and Witchcraft Book

PARENTING

Everything® Baby Names Book
Everything® Baby Shower Book
Everything® Baby's First Food Book
Everything® Baby's First Year Book
Everything® Birthing Book
Everything® Breastfeeding Book
Everything® Father-to-Be Book
Everything® Father's First Year Book
Everything® Get Ready for Baby Book
Everything® Getting Pregnant Book
Everything® Homeschooling Book
Everything® Parent's Guide to Children with Asperger's Syndrome
Everything® Parent's Guide to Children with ADD/ADHD
Everything® Parent's Guide to Children with Autism
Everything® Parent's Guide to Children with Dyslexia
Everything® Parent's Guide to Positive Discipline
Everything® Parent's Guide to Raising a Successful Child
Everything® Parent's Guide to Tantrums
Everything® Parent's Guide to the Overweight Child
Everything® Parenting a Teenager Book
Everything® Potty Training Book, $9.95
Everything® Pregnancy Book, 2nd Ed.
Everything® Pregnancy Fitness Book
Everything® Pregnancy Nutrition Book
Everything® Pregnancy Organizer, $15.00
Everything® Toddler Book
Everything® Tween Book
Everything® Twins, Triplets, and More Book

PERSONAL FINANCE

Everything® Budgeting Book
Everything® Get Out of Debt Book
Everything® Homebuying Book, 2nd Ed.
Everything® Homeselling Book
Everything® Investing Book
Everything® Online Business Book
Everything® Personal Finance Book
Everything® Personal Finance in Your 20s & 30s Book
Everything® Real Estate Investing Book
Everything® Wills & Estate Planning Book

PETS

Everything® Cat Book
Everything® Dachshund Book, $12.95
Everything® Dog Health Book
Everything® Dog Book
Everything® Dog Training and Tricks Book
Everything® Golden Retriever Book, $12.95
Everything® Horse Book
Everything® Labrador Retriever Book, $12.95
Everything® Poodle Book, $12.95
Everything® Pug Book, $12.95
Everything® Puppy Book
Everything® Rottweiler Book, $12.95
Everything® Tropical Fish Book

REFERENCE

Everything® Car Care Book
Everything® Classical Mythology Book
Everything® Einstein Book
Everything® Etiquette Book
Everything® Great Thinkers Book
Everything® Philosophy Book
Everything® Psychology Book
Everything® Shakespeare Book

RELIGION

Everything® Angels Book

All Everything® books are priced at $12.95 or $14.95, unless otherwise stated. Prices subject to change without notice.